Heaven Sent and Bent

René Steelman

Grayson-Hyde Publishing

www.SteelmanFamilyFoundation.org

Grayson-Hyde Publishing
Portland, OR
ISBN: 9780692640562
Library of Congress Control Number: 2016933193
Printed in the United States of America
First Printing 2016
Cover Design by David Redonsense
Editing by Gwen Hoffnagle and Peggy Lee Hanson
Cover Photo by Colleen Cahill, Cahill Studios

Advance Praise for
Heaven Sent and Bent

René Steelman takes us into the pain and laughter, the courage and soulfulness of motherhood, as one who has been there and done that, both valiantly and humanly. And there's more here: a lovely guide to living a spirit-centered life in the midst of busy days and trying circumstances. I couldn't put it down.

~Victoria Moran, author of *Creating a Charmed Life* and *Shelter for the Spirit*

Every child is a gift, but sometimes not the one we expected. How can we love and laugh in the face of life's surprises? René Steelman has some answers!

~Lenore Skenazy, founder of the book, blog and movement, *Free-Range Kids*

I absolutely loved reading René's story and how she has dealt with life and the joys and challenges that have come her way. It is so refreshing to hear a woman speak from her heart and be REAL! René is genuine, funny, incredibly talented, giving, and always learning. I have learned so much from her example.

~Becky Ballard, friend, wife, mother, and two-time cancer survivor

Dedication

I dedicate this book to my two amazing daughters and six beautiful and wise-beyond-their-years granddaughters. Watching my daughters mother with every instinct and gift God has given them is a wondrous site to behold. They have taught me so much and I am humbled that Heavenly Father gave me these valiant spirits. It was a risky move, but again he saw me for my possibilities and not for my reality.

Introduction

Let me tell you a story that my husband and I laugh about now but at the time was not so funny. We had just had our first child and moved into our very first little home. One afternoon I was sitting on the floor of our closet, organizing and cleaning, when my husband walked in from work and handed me a blue velvet box. His eyes sparkled as he said, "Here, this is for you." I gasped! I was literally breathless with surprise and anticipation.

The velvet nap gave the box color variations that ranged from electric blue to midnight. The box was divided in half by a shiny silver band with a tiny knob at the front just large enough to place your thumb against to gently push the box open. When he saw my delight, my joy, he suddenly panicked! "Don't open it," he yelled.

Too late. I opened the box and found... a silver belt buckle. I wasn't sure if I should pretend to be grateful for this odd cowboy accessory or if I should rush him to the hospital for previously undetected brain damage. He sheepishly explained that someone at work had given it to him and he thought it would be "funny" to play a practical joke on me and give it to me as a surprise gift. I wasn't amused.

Much like this gift, the new baby I delivered thirty years ago was packaged beautifully. He even had a cleft chin like mine. He was perfect. But also like the blue box, what was inside this baby was all wrong.

Have you ever heard the saying "Heaven sent and hell bent"? I've always thought that phrase spoke about me, a daughter of our Heavenly Father who is fiercely determined to live her life independently. However, when my son TJ was born, that phrase took on a new meaning for me. TJ is a divine gift, but his body is bent and imperfect. I am his bent and imperfect mother.

What about you and your family? Is it a little bent and imperfect like mine? Good; then you are in the right place! This book is for every woman who has struggled, laughed hysterically while holding back tears, and done everything possible to care for her children.

It is my hope that you'll find inspiration, new ideas, and more strength for the most important job in the world, mothering. I've created an easy journal for you to download and use as you read this book to help you apply the information to your life. Download it for free, as my gift to you, at www.steelmanfamilyfoundation.org/readergift.

Table of Contents

CHAPTER 1

Peek-a-Boo

I see you. I see your tired eyes in the grocery store. I see the frustration you try to hide when your toddler runs away in the park and won't come back. I also see the way your eyes light up with pride when you watch your son on the basketball court or see your daughter stick her landing during her gymnastics routine. You are the mom and have the hardest job in the world. You may feel invisible, ignored, and unappreciated. I see you and I see frustration and heartache—the heartache that this gift of bearing and raising children in a world such as we have today is more challenging than in any previous generation.

Being a mother is the most important job on the planet, and one of the most difficult; so decreed in the eighties by Oprah Winfrey. We all knew this, but somehow having the Queen of TV anoint us gave us power. That mantle, which was meant to celebrate and acknowledge women who had no other career but child care, created a generation of women who now took their role as mother to a strange level, one that involved a hidden boardroom of sorts and a ladder of progression only seen in the corporate world. Suddenly women had permission to not return after allotted maternity leave. They could hold their heads up and declare, "I AM A STAY AT HOME MOTHER, hear me ROAR!" It might have sounded like a high-pitched demand to a three-year-old, but it was meant to be a power-ROAR!

However, the sword of motherhood, tapped gently on each shoulder, has created a frustration and confusion never before seen. Mothers in the past didn't expect recognition or applause for choosing to raise the children they bore. Okay, admit it, there has always been a tinge of competition: who baked the best pies or created the sharpest creases in their kids' pressed playclothes. The greatest award, highly coveted, was first place for the mother of the child who had the cleanest underwear, declared so by the attending physician in that random emergency room after the accident that would never occur.

I will be quoting one of my favorite authors quite a bit. Ann Morrow Lindbergh's words are eloquent and timeless. On the subject of motherhood she says:

> With a new awareness, both painful and humorous, I begin to understand why the saints were rarely married women. I am convinced it has nothing inherently to do, as I once supposed, with chastity or children. It has to do primarily with distractions. The bearing, rearing, feeding and educating of children; the running of a house with its thousand details; human relationships with their myriad pulls—woman's normal occupations in general run counter to creative life, or contemplative life, or saintly life. The problem is not merely one of *Woman and Career, Woman and the Home, Woman and Independence*. It is more basically: how to remain whole in the midst of the distractions of life; how to remain balanced, no matter what centrifugal forces tend to pull one off center; how to remain strong, no matter what shocks come in at the periphery and tend to crack the hub of the wheel.
>
> —Anne Morrow Lindbergh, *Gift from the Sea*

How to remain whole—that is what we ask. In spite of the false road to the gold medal of motherhood, there are still no raises, corporate expense accounts, vacation days, or government-mandated restrictions on work hours. Motherhood, although declared tough, is harder than ever. Confusion has replaced confidence. Competition has created uncertainty. The message of equality has created an unclear definition of what being a mother really means and what this job actually entails.

I've been a mother for a long time. In fact, the duties of being "Mother" have hung on way longer than I expected or ever desired. I'm ready for the gold watch (just make sure it's an Apple watch) and the retirement party. My husband got his; where are mine?

My journey as a mother has been nothing at all like what I expected when I was a young bride. It's been joyful, rewarding, difficult, discouraging, and endless. It began with a perfectly natural birthing of a beautiful, flawless, strong boy who walked at nine months. My birthing journey ended with a difficult, stressful, emergency caesarian, giving birth to a boy who was not strong or flawless. He was struggling to breathe, never to be ambulatory—a child who is flawed physically but has secured his place in heaven as earthly perfection has been attained. TJ was born with a diaphragmatic hernia, and after a stressful birth was stricken with cerebral palsy. His existence has been miraculous and wonderful, and has become the foundation for my faith more than anything else in my life.

This book is my testimony to the power of stubborn mothers who love their children and want the best for them, no matter what. It's my way to share what I've learned about being a mother who loves to hug and cuddle but has steel in her backbone. I want to inspire you, to empower you, and to give you strength for those days when everything seems to go wrong—most days.

I believe that raising children today is more difficult than in any past generation. The world is plagued with school shootings, chemicals in our foods, and a tenuous economy. More kids are being diagnosed with autism, ADHD, and other disabilities. You have constant pressure to look like a supermodel, have perfect children, and spend hours creating homemade meals and crafts designed by

Satan himself disguised as an app called, lovingly, "Pinterest." It's impossible!

Nobody has perfect children, in spite of false claims and Facebook posts. Few of us can sport a baby bump like the supermodel Gisele. Most of us carry our babies in places other than our tummies and are void of professional makeup artists and airbrushing.

My purpose in writing this book is to share my trials; to be honest about my shortcomings and my sorrow as well as my joy; to remind mothers of what it means to be a stay-at-home mom.

First off, right away, let's clarify… it means that you rarely get to stay home! It means that you have to shelve those amazing Steve Madden boots because if you wear them you will fall and look ridiculous. I know, I've tried it. Fortunately my fall took place in my garage with no one around to laugh and judge. Six-inch heels are too much of a challenge with a baby strapped to your chest, another in a backpack, and pushing a stroller. Stroller is a misnomer by the way. Who strolls? Nannies stroll. If you have a nanny, you can wear your boots.

You know the mom I want to celebrate? The one who has an autistic child and is not afraid to show the world what a tantrum really looks like and endure the stares of unexperienced eyes; the mother of the teen who isn't in any extracurricular activities and is barely passing algebra; the mother whose child is held back from kindergarten or kicked out of preschool for biting.

There are no perfect children or perfect mothers. What a relief! Movies, television, and social media have painted a picture of motherhood that is impossible for most of us to live up to. I'm here to tell you that you can throw all those ideas of perfection out the window. I have never been perfect, nor have my children. I'm perfectly imperfect, and so is my family. If you can find a perfect family, there is a battery pack somewhere, I promise.

In this book I'm going to tell you the truth about motherhood; to rejoice with you and cry with you and realize with you what motherhood is. When the chips are down, Mom picks them up. It doesn't matter if you are exhausted, stressed out, or have the flu. As a mother you are responsible for the well-being of your children even when that burden truly feels as though it is too heavy to carry. News flash: sometimes you are given more than you can handle. Put that cliché to bed, please.

My words will not be empty words of encouragement based on idealist platitudes and happy endings. That is not reality for most of us. My stories are based on real-life experiences requiring more faith and courage than I ever realized I had. We've all seen the TV shows and movies showing how much harder things were for mothers in, say, 1845. Guess what? We are enduring a lot here in 2016. I want you to have strength for your journey as a mother and to feel that your journey is as relevant and contemporary as the latest hair style. What is the trend for 2016? In my many years of being a mother I've learned that three ingredients are absolutely necessary:

1) A sense of humor

2) A stubborn belief that you can figure things out and solve the challenges that come up

3) A deep faith that if you can't solve those challenges, Heavenly Father will provide strength and solutions. You have to act on the solutions!

Come with me as I share true stories about mothering—mine and those of some extra-ordinary women. I promise to be honest and tell you my truth—the good, the bad, and the ugly. Get ready to laugh with me and maybe tear up a little, too. It's okay. Mothering is a job that requires a heart that can hold sorrow and joy at the same time.

The stories I share of my personal trials and those of other women I've interviewed for my online blog may be difficult to read. I don't want pity, nor do the women you'll read about. Our trials are our own. Instead, we want to inspire you. Read this book with an open mind and a light and grateful heart. Receive the stories' gifts of inspiration and encouragement.

Even though you might want to devour the content in one sitting, there might be passages that have profound meaning for you and it becomes difficult to continue. When that occurs, stop, put the book aside on the table or down in your lap, and take a moment to breathe in what you just read. You might want to write down your thoughts in a journal. Let the stories and their messages sink in.

Make this book your new best friend and have a conversation with it. Best friends often help you overcome the problems you face. After reading this book in its entirety, you might not agree with everything I suggest. But if you've ever visited a therapist or know someone who has, you know that sometimes the smallest bit of advice can rub you the wrong way yet be the answer needed to get you on track. Being accountable, practicing acceptance, or taking responsibility for your behavior could be one of those tidbits of aggravation.

No one gives you a performance review for motherhood. You don't get a report card that tells you where you need to study harder or which classes you have aced. This lack of objective feedback leads us to compare ourselves to the other mothers in the neighborhood who have thinner thighs, children who are better students or athletes, or husbands who have bigger salaries. These comparisons are dangerous and harmful. I'm lucky in a way. When people see me pushing TJ in his wheelchair, it's obvious he has special needs. People open doors for us, want to help, and are often very kind. If your child has a learning disability, mental illness, or is just having a bad day, you will feel the weight of disapproving stares when they act out, flunk a class, or get caught shoplifting. These kinds of challenges can happen in any family, and they can happen in yours even when you've done everything right as a mom.

This book is for you, the tired, frazzled, delighted, and thankful mom; the mom who loves her child so fiercely she's willing to take on the world to make things better; the mom who secretly wants to run away from home some days just to have a few hours of peace. Whether your family tree looks perfect or looks a little bent, like mine does, you are welcome here.

Let's talk.

CHAPTER 2

Leopard-Print Tights at the Temple

My husband, Tony, is a very good man. He is careful, thoughtful of others' opinions, and very conservative. He's been heavily involved in our church for as long as I've known him. He cares a lot about our family and what other people think. Poor Tony, married to a woman who is outspoken, doesn't care what other people think, and isn't afraid to wear leopard-print tights to the temple! I'm a bishop's wife—I should keep my mouth shut, but I just can't!

I was having lunch with a woman I'd met through my business who was not a member of the Church of Jesus Christ of Latter-Day Saints (LDS). She said, "René, can I ask you a tacky question? All the women I've met who are members of your church are so perfect. They are in good shape, stunning, well dressed, with great makeup and hair, and have exceptional children. How does that happen?"

I started to laugh and asked her, "Where exactly are you seeing these so-called perfect Mormon women? If you are judging the entire membership by Ann Romeny's latest Christmas photo, please remember they probably had stylists and assistants! Mormon women come in all shapes, sizes, and colors!" Of course I had to share some of my many imperfections, like the fact that I hate crafts, feel sorry for myself, often swear, and have children who are not perfect but I love with all my heart. But I am a bit of a non-conformist.

There is a unique culture found in cities with a large number of LDS families, and I admit that they are usually a good-looking bunch! Clean-living folks! But that culture can cause a lot of stress. I remember being at the hospital when my daughter was having her first baby in Salt Lake City. There was a lady there with her family who had just given birth to twins. They were in the natal intensive care unit. This new mother—this woman who had just delivered *two* babies—was in a little pink jogging suit that was probably a size zero. Jogging suits are not forgiving, and there was no baby pouch or extra muffin top hanging anywhere. It was a wonder to behold!

Being of like mind often causes LDS women to follow trends that have somehow been sanctioned by an unknown higher power. Who is this Chevron Pattern God? Why must a trend be taken to such a celestial level?

So, yes, I told my friend, Mormons do have a certain look, but it is usually a regional distinction and certainly not a worldwide archetype. I live in the Pacific Northwest, and the Mormons here blend in pretty well—not as many Scandinavian and British ancestors as in the Salt Lake City area, so not as many blonds. We look different individually, but we are the same in purpose and commitment. We women can be very competitive in a subtle way. We try to be as perfect as we can be, and have perfect families. Everybody verbalizes that that's not a meaningful goal, but underneath there's still that pride that comes when your posterity is following the outlined path. You feel like an outsider when your parenting skills are being rated based on your children's use of their free agency—something we fought for in the pre-existence.

What is perfection? What is the perfect parent time line that you can follow as your children age, progress, and become adults? You don't have to be perfect to be a daughter of God. In fact, there is no way you can ever be perfect on this earthly plane. Your kids will never be perfect either. Isn't that a relief?

We want to be the best we can be and help our children grow up to be their best as well. When I was a young wife, I wanted to have eight perfect children who grew up to be assets to the church and to the world. I was young and foolish, assuming it would be pretty easy to accomplish if I dragged their little tushes to church and plopped them in the pews every week. We fumbled at family home evenings weekly (bi-weekly?), followed the manual, sang the songs, and attended the gatherings.

Women have so many opportunities to doubt ourselves, beginning with the moment we get up in the morning and look in the bathroom mirror. We see the flaws in our skin, don't like our hair, and think we are too fat or that we don't have anything to wear that doesn't look dumpy. Men have it so easy! They hop in the shower, shave, throw on a tee shirt, pair of jeans, and a baseball hat and off they go. They look great. Only teenaged females can pull that off; men seem to be able to pull off the schoolboy look for way longer.

On one hand we tell ourselves to accept ourselves as we are; we embrace our curves. But we secretly never really thought our lives would be so hard and so much would be expected of us. We believe in free agency—the idea that Heavenly Father gives us choices. Free agency is great when children are young and you dole out the free agency as you see fit. The line I always used with my kids was, "You do have a choice. You can go to bed happy or sad. But either way, you're going to bed." I gave them that free agency choice in many circumstances! Then suddenly your kids are adults and use their free agency to get tattoos, date unsavory people, or leave the church. It's a lot harder to embrace someone else's free agency, especially when their choices shatter your illusions of a picture-perfect life.

I can be judgmental. Thankfully I was given a son who would never be perfect, who has taught me to be more accepting and open. If you want to dye your hair pink and purple, that's cool with me. If you have a child with Tourette's syndrome who's cussing loudly at the movie theatre, I'm going to look at you with compassion instead of condemnation. TJ taught me that perfection isn't the goal of my life.

Did you get a patriarchal blessing? Did it turn out the way you expected?

I have a son who is not active in the church at all, yet his patriarchal blessing told him that he will be a great leader in the church. It was even as defined as to say, "You will be a bishop someday." Well, the ironic part is that he is a very successful businessman and everywhere he goes or has worked he is respected and promoted. He is loyal, honest, and hardworking. He is compassionate and kind. He is a successful young man. People love him. He has this leadership quality that you would never guess he had because he's quiet and a tad introverted. So he really is still fulfilling his patriarchal blessing. He's not an active member of the church, but that hasn't denied him the strengths he was promised. He was given an outline for how he could use those talents if he chose to. He is young, he is wonderful, but his blessing was not a fortune. It was a promise and a peek into what could be. It wasn't a reflection of my parenting or anything to do with me. It was for him.

My daughter's blessing was also very specific, stating callings that she would hold someday and how she would be a blessing to others. Her testimony is strong and she is holding to her covenants. She is the leader she was told she would be. My other children are realizing many of the blessings that they were promised, and it is such a testimony to me that they were given to me to raise, protect, and train. But they are their own people and they have all used their free agency.

When it was time for TJ to get his blessing, the patriarch said, "I have to tell you… I prayed and I fasted and I worried. I've never given a blessing to a handicapped, disabled person before."

I took it so for granted. I hadn't thought about the extent of the faith and testimony this man used to lay his hands on TJ's head and tell him of his personal blessings from our Heavenly Father. TJ was told that he was watched over from the other side by people who understand his pain and frustration, and that he would be a great blessing to his family.

I can tell you that today he, too, is fulfilling his talents and gifts. Somedays I joke with him when I put him in bed and say, "Hey, you know those people watching over you from above? Could they take over tonight and stand watch? Tell them to adjust your blankets and the amount of cool air tonight; I'm tired." He just laughs. I'm sure he knows more than he can tell me.

Whether you have your patriarchal blessing or not, whether you own a bubble necklace or sport trim thighs, whether you have a houseful of perfect children or struggle with infertility, whether you are happily married or a single mom, you don't have to be perfect or conform to other people's expectations for you or your family. We have to use our own faith and seek our own inspiration and comfort. We have to make choices, and many will be a little bent. We might have to go back and take that other fork in the road.

At the same time, strive to be kind to your sisters, both those in church and those outside of your faith. Being a mother is hard enough without our ganging up on each other. I heard a British author say once that he was very confused by the term *dysfunctional family* that we Americans use, saying, "In England we just call that family!" Every family is messy in one way or another. The mess might be publically displayed or carefully hidden behind closed doors, but there is not a single perfect mother or family on this planet.

Take a deep breath, relax, and know that you are loved just as you are in this moment. Heavenly Father has you and your family in His hand and will never drop you.

CHAPTER 3
TJ's Story

You've read a little bit about my youngest son, Tony Dean Steelman Jr.—otherwise known as TJ. Before I became pregnant with him, I suffered a miscarriage. I wasn't advised to wait at least three months after my miscarriage before trying to conceive again. As is usual for me, my attitude was, "Well, that didn't work. Try, try again." And the next month I was pregnant. Rather than going to an obstetrician/gynecologist with this next pregnancy, I saw a general practitioner—a family practice doctor—Dr. Miracle. Seriously! That was his name! One day Dr. Miracle said to me, "You're measuring large. Would you like to have an ultrasound?"

I had no idea. In my heart I hoped an ultrasound would show that I was having twins. I just thought, *Oh my gosh! This is so exciting!* Ultrasounds, back in the early eighties, however, were new and unusual for diagnosing problems. "I don't know. What do you think? You're the doctor."

"Well, I think we're okay." And he didn't move forward with the test.

I have a picture of when I was about four or five months pregnant, and I looked like I was about eight months pregnant. But everything seemed to be going along fine. The baby was due December 23rd.

On December 4th, my water broke, yet it wasn't only water. I started gushing blood. Because I previously had five natural childbirths with no complications, no medication, popping the babies out and taking them home afterward, I was innocent and naive as to what the blood signified. *It's just a little bit of blood,* I thought. *No big deal.*

I was still gushing blood when we got to the hospital emergency room. I was now sitting on towels to soak up the liquid. The doctors decided to place an internal monitor on the baby to watch the baby's vital signs, but they couldn't figure out what the problem was—the baby's heart rate wasn't that bad. Finally one of the doctors made the decision to do an emergency Cesarean section. I thought that was a great idea.

I was so excited! I was sure it was a girl, completing my perfect combo of three boys and three girls. *This baby will soon be here! This is going to be great!*

Because it was an emergency Cesarean, I was given a general anesthetic to completely knock me out. The staff was not sure what complications they were in for. When I woke up after the C-section, my husband said, "Honey, it's a boy. We had another boy. But he has a little bit of a problem. They're going to take him up to Oregon Health and Science University (OHSU) to do surgery."

I remember thinking, still out of it, *Well, that's great. Do whatever you need to do. I'm going to go back to sleep now. Just bring him back when you're done.* After a moment I thought, *I don't have problems. I don't have babies who have issues. So what's the deal?* Eventually, of course, I became coherent and better able to understand what was going on.

When TJ was born he looked fine, yet turned blue right away. He was given oxygen, but as soon as the oxygen was taken away he would turn blue. An x-ray machine was brought in to determine what was going on. The doctors saw what they called a diaphragmatic hernia, which meant TJ had a hole in his diaphragm. All of his intestines were lying up in his chest cavity. Because his internal organs had moved into his chest, there had been little space for his lungs to develop. One lung was fully developed; the other was just a little bud, a little lung bud.

The surgical plan was to put his intestines back where they belonged, close the hole in his diaphragm, and get his lung working.

When the nurses wheeled TJ into my room before his hospital transfer, they said, "You know, he has probably a twenty percent chance of survival."

Reality finally set in. I had never held him or touched him. I noticed he had a cleft in his chin like me. He was beautiful. And soon he was wheeled away.

Then I was in one hospital and TJ was in another, with all the wonderful specialists that this teaching hospital had to offer. When I was finally able to go see him, he was this tiny, perfect baby with tubes and monitors everywhere. During one of my visits the nurse wanted to turn him over onto his tummy. When he picked him up, the chest tube ensuring that no water accumulated in his lungs fell out. The staff didn't want me to see this horrifying scene and wanted me to leave. TJ was immediately rushed back into surgery.

The down side of a teaching and research hospital is the number of different doctors coming in and out and all wanting the story of his birth retold. One doctor said, "He's fine. Just treat him like a normal baby. Do whatever you do. But you need to come see me every week, as we need to keep an eye on him." Then another doctor said, "He's fragile. Don't take him out in public. When you come to the office, come in through the back door. Don't go to church. Don't go anywhere." I chose to heed the doctor who told me to treat him like a normal baby. If quarantine had been the consensus among all the doctors, I would have done as I was told, but because I had five other children, keeping him quarantined was not possible.

Because my original doctor was a general physician, a pediatrician was called in to care for TJ after he was released from the hospital ward to the pediatric ward. I think he was quite afraid that we had a lawsuit on our minds, because he kept insisting that this baby who refused to eat and cried constantly was just fine. He kept saying things such as, "He was premature, and when you consider his development you have to deduct the difference in time between when he was born and when he was due."

To that point I kept saying, "TJ was three weeks early, and he weighed six pounds, so I don't think he can be considered premature. That he's not eating and cries all the time can't be chalked up to a premature birth. I think there's something wrong."

The doctor just kept saying, "No, no, he's just premature, and that's why he's having a hard time sucking and cries all the time."

We hoped answers would be found and we could take TJ home by Christmas, but that wasn't to be. Shortly after Christmas they did an EEG on his brain to see if there had been any brain damage. We received a call to come back in for the test results. Tony was away in Seattle and unable to hear the results in person. When I arrived at the hospital, I asked the doctors if TJ would have a slight learning disability out of all of this. They looked at me as if I, too, possibly had brain damage.

"Where's your husband?" asked the one doctor.

"He's working up in Seattle," I responded.

"Well, we'd really rather talk to both of you."

"That's not possible, so what have you got?" I wasn't expecting anything to be wrong, even though TJ was lying in the hospital with tubes everywhere and wasn't opening his eyes.

The doctors were using every delay tactic they could think of. "Coffee anyone?"

Oh, this is not going to go well. "No, I'm good."

"Well, we did the EEG and actually did find brain damage. The area around his ventricles is enlarged, and that's not a good sign. And while we don't really know what that all means, he is at a very high risk of having cerebral palsy. We don't know in this instance for certain, but we feel it will be all right for you to take him home soon."

I drove home in a state of shock, leaving TJ there again. When I heard "cerebral palsy," my mind went to the only knowledge of cerebral palsy I had. Years before there had been a young man in our congregation who was about the same age I was at the time—eighteen or so—who had cerebral palsy. I remember he had a hard time talking and that it was very difficult to understand him, plus he spoke rather loudly—and he slobbered. He came to a few of the youth dances held at the church, but of course he was never going to dance. Whenever I saw this young man, I felt so sorry for him.

Back in those days you didn't see anyone who had cerebral palsy or handicaps of any kind. Families who had children who were disabled kept them hidden at home. I did not know of anyone else who had cerebral palsy, so I had no understanding of the condition except for the slobbering and difficulties communicating. All I could envision when the doctors told me that TJ might have cerebral palsy was that young man from church.

I was crying. "God, you can't do this. Give me something else. I'll take blind. Tell me he's deaf. Tell me he's going to have a limp. I don't know what, but I'm not doing cerebral palsy. The doctors did say they weren't sure, right? That TJ is just at high risk for cerebral palsy and they will keep an eye on him? Okay, then. He's going to be fine."

When we finally took TJ home, he was having trouble breathing even though he was on oxygen. He wouldn't eat. He couldn't eat. When I did get food into him, he choked and gagged. He'd constantly cry because he was hungry, so I took him to the doctor. He told me to cut a hole in the nipple and pour the food down his throat if I had to.

I cut a hole in the nipple as the doctor suggested. I tried to give TJ just a little bit, like he was a little bird, and he gagged and choked, formula going everywhere. Stupid doctor.

Eight months went by and my son was still practically starving. So I called United Cerebral Palsy. I explained everything that had happened and that I was told my baby might have cerebral palsy. They sent me an information packet. In one of the brochures was a list of things to look for if you think your child might have cerebral palsy. One of the items on the list—and I'm not sure why I only remember this one—was if they don't return your smile. We would play with TJ and tickle him, and nothing. We didn't get any reaction whatsoever. We kept looking for a reaction—a smile, a giggle, a laugh—but nothing.

Also in the packet were names of doctors who specialized in cerebral palsy. I called one of the doctors at Good Samaritan Hospital in Portland and made an appointment. Tony and I both took TJ. We walked in the door and the doctor said, "I can tell you right now, just looking at him, that he has cerebral palsy. That's very obvious. Why haven't your other doctors said anything to you?"

I explained that the one doctor was afraid we were going to sue him so he just kept making it out like everything was okay and things would be fine. And that the other doctor was an idiot who had had his license taken away since caring for TJ.

The doctor examined TJ and said, "I'm sorry to tell you this, but your son is quite severely affected."

"Okay, good to know. Now we know what we're working with."

The doctor questioned our calm acceptance. "Why aren't you more upset?"

I responded, "Obviously there's something wrong because he's eight months old now and not doing what normal eight-month-old babies do. I've been telling Tony I thought there was something wrong, but he would say, 'No, he's fine, he's fine.' So having it confirmed that there is something wrong is validating and a relief."

Now that TJ had finally been diagnosed, we were able to put a plan in place. We began right away with a speech therapist. After the initial evaluation, she found that he didn't know how to suck and then swallow. He would suck, suck, suck, and then try to swallow everything all at once. That's why there was all the gagging and choking. She suggested thickening his formula so he could drink very, very slowly. We started adding oatmeal to his formula. Finally, after eight months, he was able to get something to eat. He started weekly physical therapy, too.

We soon found out he was allergic to milk and put him on a soy formula. We had thought he had asthma, and he was on nebulizer treatments, but all along it had just been the allergy to milk.

One thing after another. But from the time we found out how to feed TJ, we were able to figure out an answer for whatever problem came next. We finally got the answers and the help we needed to care for him.

TJ is our fourth son, our sixth and last child. When he was born at the beginning of the Christmas season of 1985, his older siblings ranged in ages from two to nine. This new baby was just another brother in their eyes. My daughters played with him and dressed him up in funny costumes. My sons wrestled and teased him as he rightly deserved, being the baby of the family. TJ was included in all our family outings except the trip to Disneyland and one other. We needed to run fast, climb high, and jump into those Disney rides with the other five, who deserved a little more one-on-one.

We have had angelic caregivers who assisted us over the past twenty-eight years, mostly people we knew from our church or through my parents. There were a few young men who gladly took him to basketball games or came off the bus with him from school and treated him like one of the gang, and I met some women who loved him as much as we did and wanted a little of his heaven to rub off on their arms. Mostly, though, while growing up, his brothers and sisters took care of him if Tony and I wanted a date night.

We found caregivers hard to come by, and they didn't stick around long even when they were great. It's tougher for us to take time away from him these days, and his care is more difficult because he has matured into a young man and we have matured into old people!

Some have asked me about our plans for his care in the future. When I quickly and assuredly respond that his siblings will care for him, some have queried, "Is that really fair? Do you really think that should be their responsibility?" The questions are considerate in tone, though they get redundant, and mostly rhetorical rather than truly questioning. Explaining to others how much TJ has meant to us and added to our lives is impossible. By a stroke of luck, most of our children have ended up living near us, and we are blessed once again with their presence, but even more by their babies!

When Tony and I escaped for a recent weekend away, we dropped TJ off at our daughter's home. Her two-year-old rushed to the door exclaiming, "Hi, TJ!" She was as excited as if he were Santa Claus. She sadly asks where he is if she doesn't see him for a few days. She wants gauze taped to her stomach like he has, and the other grandkids fight over who gets to push his chair and feed him. His loud, startling laugh doesn't bother them, and when it upset another child at a store one time while we were all out, they couldn't figure out what the big deal was.

My daughter who has four children gladly welcomes TJ to their home to continue the lessons of loving one another, serving one another, helping those who can't help themselves, and not fearing others who look different, sound different, and yes, slobber.

My other son and his wife step in to help as well. Their seventeen-month-old loves to climb on TJ's chair and grab his bent and spastic hands. She loves his soft hair and wants to kiss him.

Is it fair? No, it's not fair that others can't have a built-in angel like we do, someone who offers the chance to practice the teachings of Jesus without even leaving our homes.

Is it the responsibility of your children to help? Yes, I think it is; just as we taught them to help the guy with the flat tire along the side of the road or the new family in the neighborhood who just pulled up with a U-Haul that needs unloading or the widow who needs her lawn mowed and her gutters cleaned out.

First Corinthians 13:13 says, "And now abideth faith, hope, charity, these three; but the greatest of these is charity."

I am grateful for being blessed with a spouse and six souls, given to me for a short period of time to learn lessons here on earth—lessons such as how to love unconditionally, how to love others more than myself, and how to serve others to feel the love that Christ has for all of us.

CHAPTER 4

I Want to Go on Maternity Leave

I find it somehow so appropriate that waking up this first day of October I can consider myself truly one of the walking dead. It probably isn't as obvious as the dead portrayed on the hit TV series—my skin continues to keep an acceptable pallor and I'm getting my gray roots touched up today to hide the fact that the color in my locks died long ago. It was a slow death, but I slipped quietly away yesterday, fading into my coma with no one the wiser.

My passage into the tunnel with no light at the end began yesterday morning. My agent called about an offer for an audition. My gut told me to turn down the invitation to once again be rejected, but obviously I love pain. What doesn't kill you makes you stronger, unless it kills you. The audition was for a woman in her sixties who looks like she swims. Not too hard, right? Heck, I have this acting thing down like DeNiro. I "act" like a lot of things 24/7. I can't swim, but do I look like I do? We will see. So far no call back.

I act like I do yoga, strutting in my yoga pants all day. "Oh yeah, I just finished an hour of warrior sun downward dog thing-a-ma-jigs and now I'm just gonna run a few errands at an appropriate in-the-zone heartbeat!" I hate yoga. I act like I eat a whole-food, plant-based diet, unless there is a cookie mysteriously within my reach. Then I look like someone set for the electric chair. Yes, I have taken a cookie off the top of the garbage! I act like I absolutely embrace the idea of being a mother for the rest of my stinking life. I don't.

I left the audition with my head bowed and was grateful it was still early in the morning so I could have the rest of the day to shake off the embarrassment of standing on my mark, holding my I.D. number, rattling off my name, and smiling for the camera… in a bathing suit. I wanted to yell, "You don't want a sixty-year-old who looks like she swims, you want a twenty-year-old who you think you can pass off as a sixty-year-old who looks like she swims, AND yes, those are my knees. I can pull up my thighs and prove it!"

Just as I sat in the driver's seat of my midlife-crisis car (hey, shut up, I can act like a soccer mom with my SUV), my phone rang. I looked at the caller I.D. and thought, *Wow, I'm so glad I was available to take this call. I have been waiting for this for months.* This call concerned a different kind of audition, and today was my make it or break it notice. I could tell immediately by the tone of her voice that it was a good thing I was sitting down. I sunk back in my seat and glanced out the window as she rattled off all the prelude garbage that sets you up for the fall. The Charlie Brown talk concluded and I thanked her in my most Oscar-winning, happy, understanding voice. If I had been hooked up to a heart monitor, this was when I flatlined. Third strike, I was out.

In July we had taken custody of our twelve-year-old grandson. We did so with enthusiasm, love, and a sense of duty. We knew it was the right thing to do. Fall would be here before we knew it, which meant school would be starting. I knew from past experience with our grandson that school was not a happy place for him. Since I now had the legal power to make decisions for him, I was determined to find a school that would accept him and turn his life around.

My grandson has ADD. Asking him to focus is like asking me to… wait, what were we talking about? Anyway, he is a terrific actor as well. He looks like a handsome, normal, twelve-year-old. You would assume by just observing him that he plays basketball or football because of his size, and if you looked at a headshot of him, you might ask him to audition for a part playing a happy twelve-year-old middle-schooler. Then he would open his mouth and speak and you would know that inside that tall, handsome body is a small child who just wants to play Minecraft all day and be left alone.

She told me they were sorry, but the evaluations from his audition at the school, a.k.a. trial day, were mixed. They would need to do more cognitive testing to determine whether he would fit in. Mind you, this was not an audition for an elite prep school. We had not applied, filled out mountains of paperwork, and opened our checkbooks for a school accepting only Harvard-bound prepubescents. This was for a school that accepted kids who "didn't fit in"; children in grades five through eight only; children who had ADHD and who ranked high-functioning on the dysfunction graph! The application process had been arduous. We had visited the school and observed kids coming and going. They were definitely misfits, but the happiest misfits I had seen. I was sure he would fit in. The staff had alluded to the fact that our guy would probably fit in, and that if he didn't make it there, he wouldn't make it anywhere.

This was the third private school to turn him down. I happened to have his file in the back seat of my car. With my heart now stopped and my life now outlined, I put the car in drive and, in my zombie state, drove to the public school he was destined to attend.

I went through the familiar motions. I had done this hundreds of times, thankfully, so I could pull it off in my zombie sleep. "Hi. I'm here to enroll my grandson." Enrolling a child in school, filling out more mountains of paperwork, deciding who would be the emergency call people, smiling for teacher conferences—here we go again.

I'm sixty-one years old; been there, done that; Hotel California—you can check in but you can never leave. The admissions lady sat at her desk, which was ninety degrees to the small desk that I sat at filling out the forms. She was listening to a quiet, Christian radio station. *I hope you're listening to the words of this song, Lady,* I thought, *'cause you're gonna need Jesus when this kid enters the building.* I had already given her the individual education plan (IEP) from his last school. It read like a Stephen King novel.

The school counselor was in house so she was there to skim over the paperwork as I filled out more. Yippie! She looked down at me as she entered the office were I was copying his shot records onto their paperwork. Why can't they just take a copy? Anyway, she opened up a page of his IEP and asked, "Have you read this? I mean, I don't know if you know how to read these things [zingggggg!], but let me find it… oh yes… here it shows that he was pulled out of class 79 percent of the time for special services." She looked at me with terror in her eyes.

"Ahhh, huh, yes, I did see that," I calmly replied. Calmly… very together. Meryl Streep has nothing on me! I wanted to scream, "I HAVE A LIBRARY FULL OF THESE STUPID FORMS, LADY. I HAD SIX CHILDREN!!!" But of course, again, remember, I am an actress.

"Well, do you know what exactly he was pulled out for?" she asked.

"No, I'm sorry, he wasn't living with us then."

She turned and walked out of the room. I think I noticed a slight hunch and a drag to her right leg. I was sure that hadn't been there that morning when she started her day.

Once again, I was told that it might take a day or two to look over his paperwork; they would call me. *Well, at least I know he can't be turned down here. It's a public school. They have to take everyone, the fits and the misfits. Just lets you know that even money can't buy you a placement in a school if they don't want you to perfectly fit in.*

I'm rethinking my previous mindset about private schools, charter schools, and any alternative schools. I think now that they should all be outlawed. I think that all children should have to endure real life in a public school. Teachers in public schools should be hired for their amazing abilities to teach children of all gifts and challenges. They should be paid according to their talent as teachers, enduring the day. And if you have a little Einstein, well, then, good for you. But he still has to sit next to an average kid. That, too, is life; which by the way, we don't get to audition for. We just G-E-T! Bravo! There will not be an encore.

Post Script: He did finally get accepted into this amazing school. It took more money for more testing, but he got in. He is doing so well—a perfect match for him. The amount of work and stress it took to accomplish this one act of finding a school for our grandson was tremendous. It was another reminder that you can't give up. You might have to stage a sit in, you might have to plop your behind on one of those awful mid-century Eames school chairs and swear to not leave until you speak to management—whatever you must do to advocate for your children, you must do.

CHAPTER 5

Me and Janet Jackson

I glance across and stare at three of my grown children sitting in the kiddie pool with their children. One of them has her arms placed on each knee of her husband's straddled legs. They are both laughing and multitasking by keeping a set of eyes on one child each while they converse. The conversation bounces between my other two children who likewise tilt their heads forward, watching babies as if they don whistles and red sweatshirts bearing white crosses, throwing their heads back with an occasional relaxed laugh. I shake my head, remembering what seems like yesterday when I was the young mother standing knee-high in the pool watching their moppet heads bob up and down yelling, "Watch me, Mommy."

I wish I could hear the dialog. I love to hear my adult children chat about their lives as siblings, their memories of returning yearly to this sunny getaway. I can't hear them, however, because I am across the pool sitting in the shade with their brother, the one in the wheelchair who can't stand to sit in the sun, who can't dip in the pool to cool off, who keeps me away from the company of my whole family. We are together but I am somehow banished outside the circle by circumstances beyond control.

Let me take you back to the beginning of this hard day. It gets tiresome "making it work," as they say—making a vacation rental work which was rented under the promise of being wheelchair accessible. I guess anything is accessible if you have enough men around to lift the wheelchair down and up the stairs. Accessible if sponge-bathing can get you by for the entire vacation because the bath chair doesn't fit in any shower or bathtub. Accessible if you just want to sit and listen to the nice man play his guitar at the bandstand; not so much if you enjoy going *inside* the boutique-like stores. Window-shopping is overrated!

The day began with my daily ritual of dressing TJ. At home I have room to walk around his bed. At home I don't have a strange, overstuffed recliner, an armless chair, two dressers, a queen-sized bed, and a TV stand to deal with in a 12x12 bedroom. I have to climb halfway onto the bed to dress him, and I barely have room to lift him up and place him in his chair. Yep, we knocked over the lamp with his feet—I forgot to mention the two bedside tables. Day five, this is getting old. Rental houses suck for the non-ambulatory.

This morning we headed to the Village, a quaint area of cafés and rental shops that try to squeeze a few more dollars out of the weary vacationers. People stroll the little shops and the ice cream salon in the evenings, not quite ready to put away the day in spite of rafting or hiking. Or they stroll in the morning, grabbing a bagel and a coffee, preparing for the busy day ahead.

Tanned and relaxed, Columbia- or North-Face-sweatshirt-clad, with hands in pockets, the residents stroll the cobblestone-like walkways and drink in every drop of mountain air. The ambiance is peaceful and welcoming, except for some reason my presence disrupts the Rockwellian scene. There are no other walkers, canes, or disabled. I can safely stay in the center of the square. It's open, but I don't dare divert.

Except… this morning, I diverted. The art fair opened this morning. I was anxious to take in this fun summer event, and my efforts to just get my son and me dressed and to the fair did not include breakfast, for me anyway. Everyone was walking around with the proverbial coffee cup, glancing at the booths that had sprung up overnight like flower carts in *My Fair Lady*.

I wanted to stroll the booths with a cup of something yummy, too. *I'll just bop in to the bakery shop and buy a semi-healthy smoothie, I* thought. To be truthful, it was the cinnamon-roll aroma that snaked through the air and grabbed my nostrils like a cow being led by its brass nose ring. I opened the door of the bakery and stood for a second glancing at the line before me. *Can I do this?* I asked myself. *Yes,* I thought. *Should I do this?* was the next thought. *No,* I confirmed. So I did.

The shop was L-shaped. The entry door was your first step that placed you in the line to order. There were a few people in front of me but enough space to accommodate the wheelchair and my body—enough space lengthwise, but not necessarily wide enough for a two-way pass-by, but kind of wide enough. This is where my "screw you" attitude gets me in trouble. *I want a smoothie/doughnut just like all of you, and _______ [fill in the curse word] you can just wait behind me or go around for all I care.*

So I push his chair in a few more feet, then I have to make a ninety-degree turn. Now his chair is blocking the fridge from which people can grab a water or soda. It would be blocked by anyone who was standing in line, but it's easier to reach around vertical legs than it is to reach around scrawny strapped-in legs surrounded by metal. A desperate mother awkwardly and over-apologetically asked if I would back up enough for her to open the sliding door and get her son a water. I did. And I backed up in the opposite direction a few seconds later when another mother awkwardly and over-apologetically asked if I could move so her son could point out the cupcake he wanted. I was blocking the cupcake cooler. "Move a little forward, would you mind?" "Move a little backward, would you mind?" "Excuse me, could I just reach around you?" Coffee shops are very intense! Might I suggest a decaf next time?

BUT WAIT! There's more! Behind the counter, which was even more crowded than in front, bustled thin (an obvious job requirement considering the size of this place), frantic teenagers trying to fill orders faster than you can say "Aaa… large, aaa… I mean *verdi.*" This isn't a Starbucks, mind you. No place to stand and wait for your cup of Joe to be handed to you in a cup clearly marked with your name: "Hanoi." Does René sound like that?

Anyway, I ordered only a soy steamer. By the time I actually got to the ordering station, I had lost my appetite and came to the realization that I was really never hungry. I was not hungry for food anyway. I was hungry to be one of the crowd. I wanted to walk around the art fair with a cup of something and casually "ooh" and "aah" over pottery, polished stone jewelry, and fancy metal creations. I wanted to be a laid-back vacationer.

She handed me my cup of warm soy milk—please, how desperate was I? I don't drink coffee or eat cinnamon rolls! I realized that I might have a problem pushing his wheelchair out of this box with only one hand. I sat my warm cup of stupid on the counter less than an arm's length away, pushed open the door with my back, pulled myself and my son out of the tunnel a.k.a. coffee shop, and the door shut. The door next to it, with the sign that read "Entrance that way →," was locked, and my drink was two inches away sitting on a shelf behind that locked door. Do I leave my son alone, parked unattended, rush in and grab the cup of milk? Do I dare take him back in? I'm not *that* crazy or defiant! Fortunately another person soon came out and I was able to grab my milk.

A lovely couple was entertaining the morning crowd with folk music at the bandstand. I pushed us over and we sat down. I needed to regroup. I sipped my soy and let the Linda-Ronstadt-like singer sooth my nerves.

TJ is fed through a g-tube. His total nutritional intake consists of six cartons of formula a day, divided up into feedings every two hours. Two hours goes by very quickly. Remember what it was like when you were a nursing mother? It's hard to retrieve your momentum when you have to stop what you are doing every two hours. He was hungry; it was time to feed him.

We left the comfort of our shaded seats. I scoured the area for a private place where I could feed him. I chose the side of a store. Not a lot of pedestrian traffic, secluded. I poured his formula into a larger container and added eight ounces of water. I attached his feeding tube to the button that extends from his stomach and began to pour his version of a soy steamer. His feeding tube holds two ounces at a time, so it's a process. I poured the last two ounces and reached back to put away the bottle in his backpack. As I reached back, his tube separated. I looked back to see formula pouring all over his lap.

Feeling rather downtrodden now, I sighed. I sighed and felt my shoulders drop, my head hang. I was defeated. I gulped back the lump in my throat and told my daughter that I would meet her at the pool. I had to go home and change his clothes. I made it back to the car before just a hint of a tear clouded my vision.

I had to take him into the rental home through the garage where there was only one step to negotiate. (I had to take him out of the house backwards through the front door where there were two steps to lower him down over.) Back to the 12×12 storage unit known as a bedroom. I changed him and got him back to the van, and we were on our way to the pool. I had foolishly transferred my pocketbook to a backpack thinking this would be more "pool friendly." Now I was standing at the front desk at the pool searching through a gazillion zippered pockets trying to find my wallet to pay for us to basically sit on a chair and watch others swim. Fifty dollars later, we were inside.

I emerged from the darkness of the check-in experience into the light of the water park. And light it was. It was now noon and the desert sun was high in the sky. What are the chances of finding an unattended umbrella to park him beneath? Zero.

My daughter-in-law finally caught sight of a family leaving the kiddie area and snatched one chair under an umbrella. Fast forward, soon my other children arrived, and we are back to the beginning of this story. If you remember, I began by telling you that I watched my kids frolic with their kids, and even joined them for a few moments, leaving my son in the shade. He would cough occasionally and I watched people sitting nearby shockingly look at him and then sharply look at me to be reassured that I was still on duty.

After a few hours I decided that for $50, we were going swimming. They had a chair meant for lowering non-walking people into the water. You might have seen one at a public pool or the YMCA. This one was placed strangely near the shallow area of the pool and right next to a little slide for kids. The area was filled with children and their parents.

I asked the lifeguards what the protocol was to use the chair. They summoned another guard who informed me that yes, the chair could be moved to another area, but it was really heavy and a pain to move. Ah huh, tell me about it. "Most people just enter the water in that spot and then swim to the deeper section of the pool," he said. Most people, as in *no one ever?*

They agreed to be helpful, and so I acquiesced. I rolled TJ over to the pool chair, they turned it on, turned it toward me, and I lifted him out of his wheelchair onto the hard plastic chair. I quickly buckled the belt and dashed to the stairs to get in the water and guide him into the pool. Mind you, these chairs are meant for people who bend at the waist, not spastic, stiff, two-by-four-shaped people. Within seconds he was in the water, and I expected him to laugh with delight and relax his stiff body in the warmth and depressurization of the water. He didn't. He didn't like it. He whined, he complained, he was even stiffer as his body was uncomfortable with the uncontrollable freedom of the water. He didn't like the people splashing him either.

I forced him to stay in for about a half hour. I didn't dare ask the kids to help me get him out just a few minutes after we got in. When I felt we had served our time, paid our penance, I motioned for the guards to release us and we floated over to the plastic chair. We had to scurry away the little ones again and a crowd began to gather. Two old ladies actually stopped and planted themselves to watch the show. Children stopped their game of Marco Polo to see the exhibition. Unaware of the spectacle that we had become, my seven-year-old granddaughter helped me buckle the strap around his waist. Since he had already experienced this nightmare just thirty minutes prior, he knew what to expect so he stiffened up even more. It was difficult getting him seated in any fashion. We did the best we could and gave the signal to lift the seat.

I ran to meet him as the lifeguards hung on to him by his life jacket. They once again turned the chair away from the pool and I crouched down to get into position to lift him off the plastic chair and back into his wheelchair. As I lifted his wet and now heavier body, I could tell that my swimsuit was going to betray me. Yes, you guessed it. I can now join the Janet Jackson and Tara Reid club. I totally flashed a nipple to the gaping crowd watching.

As soon as I could release my hands from his body I pulled up my swimsuit and carried on as if nothing had happened. I took off his life jacket, replaced his tee shirt, and we walked back to the kiddie pool as if we did this every day. My chattering granddaughter by my side, no worse for the experience, was gleefully asking me if I could go back and go swimming with her. I wanted to, I couldn't, and I wanted to go home.

That is what it is like if I leave the comforts of my home and venture out into the cruel world—the world that may have a sign that says, "Handicapped Parking," but not for wheelchairs. The world that legally now lowers a curb but still crams every aisle of a store with items to sell to non-handicapped consumers who can circumnavigate the mess. The world that sets in place a wonderful device meant to look as if it could assist non-ambulatory sunbathers in taking a refreshing dip in a pool, but actually is a hassle for the lifeguards and only assists a few far and a few between. Looks good though.

I've always loved to travel. I left home at eighteen to see the world, and I did. At the age of thirty-two my wings were clipped by the birth of TJ, and my travels have never been the same. Now I just want to stay home. It's easier. I make myself leave, to get off the couch, to disturb his relaxed slumber, because I know it's good for both of us. But is it? I feel like today was pretty life-threatening and humiliating. Which is worse, a flat butt from sitting on the couch or the memory of flashing a nipple in front of a crowd?

Ask me tomorrow.

*"Don't wish me happiness. I don't expect to be happy all the time...
It's gotten beyond that somehow. Wish me courage and strength and
a sense of humor. I will need them all."*

—*Ann Morrow Lindbergh*

CHAPTER 6
Let's Talk about Men

The greatest gift my mom gave me was a good man for a father. Not the man who biologically fathered me—he gave me straight teeth and thick hair. The man I call my father came a few years later. This man installed etiquette, no elbows on the table, "May I be excused?" from the dinner table, Broadway tunes, Elaine May, Mike Nichols, and Julie London. He taught me that your word is a contract and that silence can say more than words. Okay, I may not have learned that piece real well, but I observed it! In him I saw a quiet man who loved unconditionally and was faithful to a fault.

My true father will not fight with my mother. When he does disagree with her, he does so silently. You only know he's angry or in disagreement because he bows his head and his face turns red. Ironically, no one else is allowed to fight with Mom either. If you do dare to disagree with her or, heaven forbid, make her cry, you will see rage pour out of this proper English man that is right up there with *The Exorcist!*

He showed me by example how a good man should love his wife. I didn't have to read a book or take a class to see how to make a marriage work.

My mother and I conspired to catch this man and keep him. We have never worked together on a project so successfully! I was only seven and Mom was twenty years older, but we made a great team. The lesson was: If you see it and you want it, you must pursue it and make it happen.

My dad was a confirmed bachelor. He had a Carmen Ghia, a stereo that he built himself, and a bachelor pad. He also had the misfortune of being tall, dark, handsome, and British. Who doesn't go weak in the knees for that accent! He was a section manager at Western Electric (now AT&T), and Mom worked in his area. She saw him, she set her sights, and then she got him.

This woman, though she was hot and a real looker, came with baggage in the form of children: me and my ten-year-old brother. I, to this day, will testify that it was the darling daughter who sealed the deal! This new father was a blessing to all of us.

In high school, I never really dated. There were a few boys I chased but they were one-sided affairs. Our church had weekly dances on Saturday to bring young people together, but there, too, I was a wallflower. After many Saturday nights standing with arms crossed and heads tilted, my girlfriend and I decided to boycott the dances altogether. They were a waste of time.

Until one Saturday after we had been out for a long bike ride. We decided, "What the heck. Let's go to the dance tonight." Past experience had taught us that sleeping in large rollers and whipping up new outfits did little to change our position against the wall. I didn't spend a lot of time figuring out what I was going to wear, applying extra eyeliner, or straightening my naturally wavy hair. And I just didn't care—I was sick and tired of getting all dressed up with no results.

As fate always has it, however, that night changed my life for eternity. There was a new guy whom I'd never seen before. He was handsome, with a haircut inspired by the Beach Boys, an electric smile, and perfectly placed Chicklet-like teeth! We danced the night away. And then he asked if I wanted to see his new car.

To this day he insists I was impressed with his new Chevy Nova. I know it was metallic brown and kind of pretty. But I really didn't care about his car—I thought *he* was pretty!

We dated the whole summer, spending the weekends together. We both worked summer jobs and had made commitments beginning in the fall. He had signed up to serve a two-year mission for our church, leaving in October. I had signed up to serve our country in the United States Navy, leaving in January.

We talked about being together in the future but didn't mention the word *marriage*. We talked about family topics as if they were possibilities in our lives as much as in anyone's future. We mentioned togetherness as much as you can when you are eighteen and both committed to being separated for no less than two years. Two years is two *hundred* years in a young brain.

Tony wanted to buy me something before he left. I suggested a ring. His confusion at my desire for a bling-thing on my left hand should have been my first sign that this guy was no Romeo and a little clueless.

"What kind of ring? You already have rings," he said. *Oh good gravy, this is not going as I thought it would.*

"Let's just visit a few stores and ah, oh, I don't know, see what's out there," I suggested. The next few dates involved jewelry stores. Mother's lesson to get my man was in full force! I had my sights set, knew what I wanted, and was pursuing it and making it happen!

The jewelry stores we visited had mostly male employees. Fortunately for me, it was football season. Therefore small, portable television sets were on and set to whatever game was playing. While Tony was distracted by the game with said man employee, I quietly asked another employee to show me to the "pre-engagement" ring section. Nobody gets "pre-engaged" anymore, but for a year or two in the seventies it was an excellent marketing tool—little rings with little diamonds with a big meaning, at least in my eyes. I found one, Tony bought it, and the jeweler put it on my left-hand ring finger. I repeat, *the sales guy gave me the ring* and the betrothed was never the wiser that he was branded, corralled, and spoken for!

Tony left for his assignment, and I left for mine. We wrote back and forth, but again, red flag number 758 appeared. I wrote about our love, our plans, a little of what I was up to, being stationed in Yokosuka, Japan, and more about our love, and by-the way—what-are-our-plans?

He wrote about his—mission.

Finally the two years were almost up, and I needed more of a commitment. I was allowed a thirty-day leave. I could go home, we could reunite, date a little, and then I would have to return to my duty station, alone. "OR...," I said, "I could go home, we could get married, and you could come back with me to Japan!"

He responded, "Okay." I don't think he was on bended knee in Indiana when he said okay. I've still not seen him on his knees unless he is praying, even after all these years. The last few months of his mission, my letters had taken on the theme of wedding plans. He didn't care. He just said, "Okay. Did I tell you about my new area? My new companion? My new assignment?"

In all fairness, Tony was a great missionary, totally devoted to his service as assistant to the mission president—moving missionaries to different districts, handling a change in the mission presidency—and not distracted by a silly girl. I had a scrapbook filled with wedding and honeymoon ideas. He had an empty checkbook and a commitment to God.

Three weeks after Tony returned home during my leave, we were married. Mind you, we hadn't seen each other in two years. We might as well have had an arranged marriage! I didn't know him, and after forty-one years, he still can't figure me out!

We spent our honeymoon night at a travel lodge in Salt Lake City, Utah, and two days visiting Tony's old companions from his mission and one of his former mission presidents. Those dreams of skiing at Park City and honeymooning in a romantic mountain retreat were soon dashed. We drove home, he went to work, and a few days later we flew back to Japan—and started our life.

I highly recommend that newly married couples fly away and spend the first year of marriage far from extended family. We didn't have to decide—or fight about—whose family we went to for the holidays or any other occasion. It was nice, but had its rocky moments, as we had to really learn who we were and how we got together—*why* we got together!

We couldn't spend days looking into each other's eyes, backpacking through Asia, or seeing the sites abroad, because we both worked, as Tony was able to get a job on base. We traveled as we could on weekends, but Tony was immediately put into the branch presidency of our tiny little group, which meant faithfully attending meetings every Sunday.

To this day, Tony is not romantic. He's not going to change, and I can't make him change. Back in the nineties there was a radio show with Dr. Laura Schlesinger, who discussed relationships with her listeners. Women who were having trouble with their men would call in to speak with Dr. Laura and get advice on how to handle the situation. If the woman described a certain demeanor or a certain way the charged man acted, one of the first questions Dr. Laura was asked was if the man had ever acted that way before. More often than not, the answer was a resounding, "Yes. But I thought I could change him after we were married."

I now look back on how Tony behaved when we were dating. On our third or fourth date we went hiking up to Multnomah Falls, a waterfall on the Oregon side of the Columbia River Gorge. He still hadn't held my hand or put his arm around me. The relationship felt like a truly great friendship. We were chattering, talking, getting along well, but no moves made on me—at all. I told my girlfriend, "Look, if he doesn't even try to hold my hand soon, I'm making the first move!"

But then, during one date, Tony and I were walking across a busy road, and he grabbed my hand. He guided me as if to say, "Here, I will protect you. You are under my stewardship now and as long as you are with me, I will protect you." From then on we didn't stop holding hands.

Tony is still very uncomfortable with public affection. He is uncomfortable holding my hand or kissing me in an elevator or a restaurant. He's never been one for keeping me under his arm when we sit at church or at an event. However, when we were dating, he would always open my door for me. He would always walk on the outside of the sidewalk or the road, and he still does that. I knew that he was shielding me, keeping me out of harm's way. And, of course, Tony always paid for everything. I just knew that he was a faithful guardian and that he was really interested in my well-being, and I felt very safe with him.

The happily-ever-after part of this fairy tale is still to be written because we aren't in the "after" part of our lives yet. Plus, the message here is that our life together has not been a fairy tale. We've had a few wicked witches, a few dragons to slay, a few years of confinement in an isolation tower, and a few fairy godmothers in the form of men with white coats. My prince charming doesn't lavish me with surprise gifts, but he surprises me with sudden declarations like "Go buy something you like." He forbids anyone to speak rudely or disrespectfully to me. He works hard and has been a good example of service and devotion to our children.

Tony is clueless when it comes to anything that might be found in a scrapbook or on a vision board. He gets excited about his checkbook balancing and tightens his jaw when mine doesn't. He is the typical male when it comes to finding something, pulling off a chore without my intervention, believing the GPS lady, and my desire to coordinate holiday clothing.

He is unusually talkative for a guy unless it's about feelings, then he's the typical male. His innate desire to be charitable often makes me worry that he will give someone in need all of our clothing, and maybe our car, but so far so good on that one.

He loves me more than air, but my feelings have often been hurt when I felt that he put the needs of others over those of our family. I know, however, that I put our family's needs over and above anyone's, so we strike a balance on that point.

In other words, being married for forty-one years has not been a story of tulips and bliss. It's been happy and sad, angry and blissful, perfect and horrid. Anyone who declares that their union has been anything but is a liar! Blending two paradigms, two personalities, two different brains, and two different sets of hormones, and adding little people to the mixture, is harder than any landing on Mars.

What we do have is unity, stewardship, leadership, and devotion. We are unified in our covenant of marriage and to our children. We are unified in our belief in our religion and all that it professes. We are unified in wanting the best for our children, grandchildren, and families.

We are NOT unified in how long our boy's hair should be, whether a white shirt is always necessary, or anything that has to do with my appearance. Tony learned early in our union that his desire to be conservative and blend in was the polar opposite of mine. He learned early on to *never* buy me clothing or comment on my style. He doesn't tell me how to wear my hair or my makeup. He doesn't think of me as an appendage of him. Tony allows me to be myself and uses that aforementioned jaw-tightening trait. We agreed early on that the inside of the house was mine, and the outside was his. I have questioned his use of planter boxes, and he has shaken his head and flinched at my use of toile and faux-painted walls.

If I could give a nugget of truth to young people embarking on the path of marriage, it would be to not burden yourselves with the casual clichés that are thrown around so recklessly, such as "Remember why you first fell in love," "Remember the good times," and "Remember your marriage vows." "Firsts" are often shrouded in unrealistic projections. We are not ourselves when we first enter a relationship; we are the best *versions* of ourselves. That facade cannot be kept up for a lifetime. Fun picnics and fancy cars have to be traded in for mini-vans and soup and crackers at some point.

If you married a man who loved his fancy car, and you have fond memories of that fancy car and the fancy dates, those memories slash the wound of reality for a man who won't give up that fancy car for three kids and French fries. If your wedding dress was a size two and your husband has fond memories of a beautiful, slim bride walking down the aisle—those are the memories that can taint a selfish spouse, especially if he can't come to appreciate how strong you have become through bearing children or surviving breast cancer.

Memories are subjective, and are never the complete truth. A recent article in *Scientific American* brought out that with time, memories not only lose their rich vividness, but they can also become distorted as our actual experiences tango with a fictional past. Researchers from John Hopkins University have come up with a new theory that memories are transformed each time we revisit them. When we recall a memory, we often add or subtract little tidbits, making the memory into a fictional account.

When I hear older married couples describe a marriage that was never troubled by disagreements, or a wife who always found favor with her husband and all the decisions, moves, job transfers, and outside interferences, I know it was a choice to nurture the story for the sake of happy memories. No one argues that choosing happiness over grumpiness is not preferred; but setting up unrealistic expectations for others—and you, yourself—is cruel and disheartening.

Our men can drive us nuts, frustrate us endlessly, and cause us lots of work and worry. They can also be our teachers, protectors, and providers. And men can be violent, angry, and selfish. It is your duty to protect yourself and your children from that behavior. Our Heavenly Father has set the example and given us written direction for loving each other, caring, and protecting our children.

When my mother left my biological father, it was unheard of in that time. My maternal grandmother loved my father and was angry at her own daughter for cutting him out of our clan. But my mother married way too young and knew that it was a union born of distress and not devotion. She knew she couldn't be married to my father and be emotionally all alone with her two children for the rest of her life. She wanted a companion, a father to her children, someone who came home willingly and wanted to be with his family.

My biological father was not a bad man. He was never violent, he was just absent. He had his own life and wanted to live it without the burden of hearth and home. He loved us in his own way, and I loved him in spite of this aspect of this character.

My mother and stepfather accepted missionaries into our home and willingly committed to a religion that is unpopular and widely misunderstood. My biological father would never have allowed this. My mother's family rejected her for many years because of her choice to join The Church of Jesus Christ of Latter-Day Saints. Some of those relationships were never mended, but some were.

The family is the basic unit of society. When our families break down, so do our communities. One of my favorite quotes is this one from Lee Iacocca: "No matter what you've done for yourself or for humanity, if you can't look back on having given love and attention to your own family, what have you really accomplished?" My mother knew what a family should look like and she was not going to stand by and let hers fail. My mother is my hero, and, for me, the greatest example of determination.

CHAPTER 7

Hold My Hand

The streets were reflective and beginning to confirm the weather warning of freezing rain. Who in their right mind would venture onto the highway at five in the evening with this impending bad weather? Well, me of course! I was a mile from the safety and warm fireplace of my home but my maniacal drive to complete every task on my to-do list prevailed.

In my car, with the radio tuned to National Public Radio (NPR), and no children, I could move quickly and with focus.

Okay. Who am I kidding? I never move with focus. I move, mind you, but my focus drifts. One time I left my naked son unattended for a minute or two while I took his clothes to the laundry room. I spied a floral arrangement in the dining room that needed adjustment. Could you continue a bathing ritual knowing that a lily was hanging too far to the left? I couldn't!

Anyway, I was heading to a Target store to meet a friend—a talented photographer I met while on my quest to get out more, meet new friends, and see the world. My new friend John was the type of person who said yes without blinking when you asked for his help, shy and reserved, but at the same time throwing himself into hectic public activities to further his craft. I was also delivering a Santa suit to him.

My journey to meet new friends began with an invitation to model clothing at a women's upscale clothing store in Portland. Joy's Uptown caters to mother-of-the-bride attire. I've had that title five or six times so I knew the store, knew the owner, and was thrilled at the invitation. That very event secured five new friends right off the bat, and my journey took flight. One gig after another and here I was in Target meeting John. We had a quick hot chocolate in the attached Starbucks, and I gave him the suit and said farewell, as the racks of clothing were calling me.

I stood for a moment after our good-byes and took a deep breath. I scanned my digs slowly, moving my eyes from left to right; having pinged at the right, beginning the pong back to left, I stopped dead center. There was a rack of clothing I had not seen before. Not in Vancouver, not in Tualatin, not at Jantzen Beach, not on a train, not in a box, not with a fox. Nowhere else had I seen this line! I held up one version of the dress in black. Hmmm. Maybe the blue. No. I put the dress back, deciding once again that I cannot wear something that would put me at risk of bumping into a seventeen-year-old with the same dress.

I meandered around, then I finally emerged from my coma and remembered I was supposed to be shopping for Christmas pajamas for the gang. I focused (stop laughing) and looked for the boys' department. It was then that I noticed an annoying noise. It sounded as if a child was searching for a parent. It was a strange call, not frantic but consistent; as if a child was separated from the parent, yet not afraid.

"Paww" or "Baaaww" I thought he was saying. Just one word, as if he were asking where his father was, full in the knowledge he was just an aisle away. After a few moments I realized the call had a rhythm that made me think it wasn't a lost child but rather an annoying brat being left to play games while his neglectful parents shopped away.

The sound echoed and shot to my ear like a sharp arrow, the rhythm adding to the unsettling sound. I couldn't concentrate now, for I was hooked on the metronome-like rhythm. I waited in time for the next yell.

I discovered that the boys' section was on level two, and was relieved. I entered the elevator and breathed a sigh that the unwatched child remained downstairs and I was heading up.

Being completely focused now, and remembering that the roads looked perilous when I had begun my trip, I reminded myself that it was getting colder. The drizzle had turned to freezing rain, and I needed to get out of the store and get home.

What with my wandering eyes did appear but the coolest designer chairs and child rain gear! I studied the chairs but my peripheral vision took in a grandma eyeing snow globes with her grandson. I heard her say, "It's called Tourette's syndrome." Her grandson asked her to explain and as she was doing so, I lost focus of the chairs and walked over to start a conversation.

Maybe I just *re*-focused or *multi*-tasked, but in any case, we discussed the "call," how loud it was, and how disturbing it was. I soon learned that her grandson, Griffin, was ten years old. He joined in the conversation and I loved him immediately! He was another version of my grandson—handsome and bright. Griffin kept saying, "I love this conversation," or "I suppose we won't meet again for ten years."

His grandmother explained that Griffin was a twin and that both twins were on the autism spectrum. Their father had only just passed away. Griffin filled in some details of his father's death with the no-emotion and odd joy for the subject that plagues people with this disorder. Grandma and I smiled and laughed along with him and I seriously wanted to take him home with me. We stood and talked for a few minutes more and I said good-bye, once again, to new friends, giving Grandma my business card and telling her to call me.

I normally wouldn't have noticed the typical northwestern-looking woman walking toward us. Her curly brown hair fell to both sides of her head, evenly following the center part. A thermal padded vest topped the jeans and boots. Small and looking every bit the Columbia-Sportswear Oregonian, she would have been a blur in my side vision had she not suddenly let out that familiar cry, "BAAAWWW!"

The three of us jumped and our heads snapped to see where this auditory assault had come from. Her sideways glance met my wide-eyed stare. We both quickly looked away.

There we were, all of us, in Target. Oregonian woman with Tourette's, Griffin with Asperger's, John with his shyness, and me with my ADHD! What a bunch! What a lot of crazy, some might say. I say, however, hooray for us! We were all Christmas shopping! We were out—out in the world, completing our list of things to do—except me, as the store didn't have any pajamas, I don't think—did they?

I climbed into the elevator, leaving what felt like a higher kingdom, and descended back to earth. A large woman with a scowl on her face joined me. Her black coat didn't hide her girth or her hunched shoulders.

"Jeesh," she blew. "That child is so annoying. I can't stand that noise," she exclaimed.

"I know," I said, "It's actually a woman with Tourette's."

The woman's face relaxed and the scowl softened, just a bit. It was an ingrained look you could tell, but relaxing the best she could. "Ba-humbug," she said. "I'm glad you told me. I was about to complain to the management."

That had been me just a few minutes before—me, on that elevator, annoyed.

Whew! I was so thankful to have been to what seemed like heaven; to have met Griffin and his grandma, making a connection with a brave soul; and to have seen the light! I hope I can wonder with compassion more from now on. Imagine, just by beginning a conversation with a stranger you can change an attitude of another. Perhaps it's just like holding hands.

One recent Sunday, when Tony and I couldn't find our two little granddaughters after church services, we weren't really worried. We knew where to look, and in the typical sea of people in any LDS chapel across the world, this was typical.

A Mormon congregation is called a "Ward" and each building is usually assigned at least three Wards. The Wards are divided geographically, and depending on where you live, you are assigned to a specific Ward, and each Ward is assigned a specific time to attend the three-hour block of services on Sunday. There can be anywhere from 600 to 900 people using the building on Sundays, alternating between classrooms and the chapel. Children meet separately from adults after the initial hour-long Sacrament meeting. They are given a lesson, sing songs, and work on subject-oriented crafts. On this particular Sunday our family had the pleasure of having our six- and four-year-old granddaughters, Elise and Emery, with us. They know the routine.

Tony agreed that I would take TJ out to the van while he rounded up the girls. Having a great parking space in front of the building provided amusing entertainment as I sat watching the doors. The double glass doors swung back and forth as people left through one side, entered through the other, and tried to enter through one side as others tried to exit that same side.

I waited for Tony to emerge with said girls in hand and soon he burst through the swarm of people, looked at me, and mouthed, "Do you have them?" I shook my head, "No." He then turned and, like a salmon ready to spawn, reentered the building.

I wasn't worried. The building contains a full-sized basketball court, and often the children run in there and play a quick game of tag with their friends. Soon Tony came out with the little girls smiling, colored pages in one hand and a treat in the other.

As he buckled them into their car seats, Tony explained that when he found them, Elise had Emery by the hand.

"She was a little scared, Papa," Elise said. "But I took her hand and she was okay."

"Aaahh, that's right." I smiled and told my husband, "When Emmie was a baby and would be upset in her car seat, Kendall would just reach back and take her hand. That calmed her right down."

Holding hands is the universal sign of love and caring, whether it's the first time you place your finger in the palm of that newborn baby or the gentle grasp of a twisted arthritic hand that needs to be steadied and secured.

I love to people-watch, and especially to watch people walk hand-in-hand—that always brings a smile to my face and I want to know their story. Sometimes I shake my head and think, *How on earth did he hook up with that hottie?* Other times I might ask myself, *Do they hold hands everywhere they go or just on their morning walks?* Or I sometimes just sigh and think, *I bet they have been together fifty years, and they're still strolling hand-in-hand.*

While spending time with my daughter in Beijing, China, and in spite of the questionable air quality, I tried to run daily. But I mostly just wanted to be among the people and take in the culture. The first thing I noticed was the handsome couples walking hand-in-hand— smartly dressed men in their overcoats and women in coordinated scarves, shoes, and designer bags. The young people varied as they do all over the world. Some had bleached blond hair. Some sported Mohawks with saggy jeans. But others had great haircuts or simple ponytails with bangs.

Public displays of affection are something new in China, however. The youngsters have taken to this new freedom quite easily, but the older people simply hold hands.

"I wanna hold your hand," the Beatles sang, and I dreamed that would happen for me someday.

"Take my hand," I told my babies, protecting them from the street traffic, the crowds at the fair, or a busy mall.

"Hold Papa's hand," I instructed my grandsons as they left for an all-boys adventure.

"HOLD MY HAND!" I demanded through clenched teeth as I labored to bring another baby into this world while my poor, helpless husband stood by my side.

Holding another person by the hand brings comfort, security, and connection. It is no wonder that references to our savior Jesus Christ are made through the works of His hands.

Three Nephi 18:36 says, "And it came to pass that when Jesus had made an end of these sayings, He touched with His hand the disciples whom He had chosen, one by one, even until He had touched them all, and spake unto them as He touched them."

Doctrine and Covenants 6:37 says, "Behold the wounds which pierced my side, and also the prints of the nails in my hands and feet; be faithful, keep my commandments, and ye shall inherit the kingdom. Amen."

Jesus is showing us physically what he has done on our behalf. "Look at my hands," he instructs us. "See what I have done, now you go and do all that you can do." He instructed through example. He promised that He will take care of us. "Behold I have graven thee upon the palms of my hands; thy walls are continually before me," says Isaiah 49:16.

The hand is a perfect example of God's creation. No two hands are the same. Every hand is unique, and only your hand can identify you. Use your unique hands to reach for the hand of someone you love. Reach your hand to pull up another who is down. Clap your hands in joy at the sight of a three-year-old dancing. Fold your hands in prayer of thanksgiving or extreme sadness. Use your hands to build, to pick up, to stroke, to comfort.

"He's got the whole world in his Hands."

"Put your hand in the hand of the Man from Galilee."

And my favorite from Jewell: "My hands are small, I know. But they're not yours, they are my own…and I am never broken."

I give thanks today for my hands, as I write these words. I notice the joints beginning to bend with age. The skin is not so soft and smooth anymore, and the dreaded spots are hiding beneath my thinning skin. But they work and I am grateful, I am grateful.

Just as Tony and I want to begin a foundation for donating handicapped-accessible vans to those in need because of the hardship we experienced with TJ, others find strength in their own trials and help those with similar needs. For example, when a friend decided to sign up for dental hygienic school, her son received the diagnosis of being autistic. Now she and her husband have a dream to start their own business through which they will get a van, fill it with dental cleaning equipment, and go to kids who have super-sensory disorders and can't sit still or find it hard to be in a regular dentist's chair. This friend is using her son's disability to serve. The hard times can provide glorious times—and hope—to other families in need.

I find that I must keep focus on how to serve my glorious family, and not give in to my own whining and complaining. Many families have much more dire circumstances than I do.

We are now holding our grandson's hand as he traverses his world, helping him find his way. It's one of the hard times. He is a kindhearted, giant man/child who has experienced more in his short twelve years than most of us ever will. In our frantic effort to "fix" him quickly, we thought music lessons would be a great way to begin summer vacation. He humored us. It wasn't his idea of summer break, however, and he did not want to go. He sat through one or two classes but then put his foot down. The teacher had too much hair on his arms, he said. The next lesson day arrived and he put up a little fight, but at least he got dressed for class. However, he came out in a sweatshirt and long pants.

I said, "Buddy, you can't wear that. It's going to be ninety degrees today. Go change your clothes."

Well, that just upset him even more. Now he couldn't wear what he wanted to wear. Then I heard doors slam. He was hiding and I couldn't find him. I thought he must have run off. Time passed and we were running late. I got in my car and drove around the neighborhood trying to find him, came back to the house, opened all the doors again, and yelled for him. I finally got back in the car, angry, frustrated, and embarrassed. I called his music teacher, "I'm not going to make it today because I can't find my grandson. He took off. He didn't want to come to piano. I've got the keyboard in the back of my car. I will bring it to you. I'm done. I'm not going to play this game."

The music teacher, Rob, who is really good at what he does, said, "I work with the special education department at the Vancouver school district. I know what you're talking about with these kids who have focus issues. What we need to do first is cut his lesson time back from an hour to a half hour. Then we need to take that focus on lighthouses he has and have him make a collage of different lighthouses. Once he has the collage made, we'll create a soundtrack—background music for him to use for his collage."

Isn't that brilliant?

Because of the work of many devoted mothers, public schools are legally obligated to include all children. Children with disabilities can stay in the school system until they are twenty-one. Once that magic birthday arrives, many young adults are without support of any kind. No one is there to hold their hand any longer. Inclusion is not a reality. There is nothing to be included in.

It was a difficult adjustment for TJ. We were both lost and alone. We figured it out and moved on, but I'm back on duty with my grandson. I have learned that the word *inclusion* does not demand or guarantee acceptance or friendships. He is legally able to attend a public school, but no one at that school is legally obligated to like him or care. Sometimes you get lucky and meet someone like Rob who understands how to reach kids like my grandson. At other times you have to become the child's advocate and stand up for their rights in receiving the help they need and do what's best for the child all by yourself.

One of my favorite quotes is from the book *Jonathan Livingston Seagull* by Richard Bach:

> Don't believe what your eyes are telling you. All they show is limitation. Look with your understanding. Find out what you already know and you will see the way to fly.

I don't know what the future holds for my grandson or anyone else in my family. I do know that I'll be there, holding their hands, for as long as I am able. That's what mothers do.

CHAPTER 8
Solutions and Silver Linings

Who am I to write a book—this book, sharing my story and the trials I've experienced in my life so far? Who am I to offer advice to you, perhaps a young married woman, or a young person who seeks answers to problems before they arise, or a much more seasoned sage? Who am I?

I've asked myself, "What am I doing? Nobody is going to read this." But when a feeling grabs hold of you and doesn't let you go, you know you just have to give in and get the task done.

Is there something you've been considering doing? A dream, perhaps, you've longed for? Maybe achieving it seems out of reach or you're afraid you'll be ridiculed and judged for your unrealistic silliness. Maybe it's not your season but you feel pressure to be all and do all before the age of twenty-nine! Who are you?

A while back I was listening to an interview with author Judy Blume, who made the comment about being a free-range child. That was the first I had heard of the phrase. But then, soon afterward, while heading to the office to do my radio show, I was listening to SiriusXM. Host Michael Smerconish was interviewing Lenore Skenazy. She had written a book back in 2009 called *Free-Range Kids*. When I heard Lenore, I thought Judy got the phrase from her. Immediately I knew I had to ask Lenore to be on my radio show.

I emailed to ask if she would be a guest the following week, and Lenore said, "Yeah, I'll give you a half hour." *Well, I will take your generous offer to me, a complete stranger, a nobody. I'll take a half hour.*

What I just shared with you was a dream of sorts. I've always wanted to write a book. I've always wanted to be a journalist and interview people and tell their stories. I also wanted to be a mother. I wanted that more. And since that job came first, my other dreams had to sit for a time.

Here is another favorite quote from *Gift from the Sea* by Ann Morrow Lindbergh:

> The sea does not reward those who are too anxious, too greedy, or too impatient. To dig for treasures shows not only impatience and greed, but lack of faith. Patience, patience, patience, is what the sea teaches. Patience and faith. One should lie empty, open, choiceless as beach—waiting for a gift from the sea.

My mother always taught me, "God gave you a mouth; use it." She didn't know I would take that advice and run with it. I think she just meant to ask for what you want in life. I took the advice as that, but also to never stop talking, which has often proven to be a mistake. Back to my dream job…

To learn more about Lenore Skenazy before the interview, I got the audio version of her book. As I listened, I realized her writing is everything I could ever hope to emulate as an author. When you listen to something that good you can't help but compare credentials! Lenore graduated from Yale. She got her master's degree from Columbia. And then she worked as a journalist for many prestigious publications such as *The New York Sun*. And that makes you start thinking, *Who do I think I am? What am I doing writing this book that no one will ever read? I don't have a degree from Yale. I'll just put the whole idea in the drawer with the two- and three-page articles I've written over the years and hide it, hopefully to be romantically discovered after my death, posthumously published, and then made into a major motion picture.*

But it's there. In the early morning hours my eyes pop open and the words begin to flow. I have to catch them before they swim away. My mind won't rest until the words are gathered in the net and dumped onto the deck of my legal pad to be sorted and frozen like a perfect New England catch. Some are returned to the waters and some must be cleaned before they are ready to be displayed at market. But I know they have to go to market. My catch has to be arranged for shoppers to judge, flip over, hold in their hands. I am the one with the slit gut now; my insides have been revealed and I am hoping my catch will end up on someone's nightstand.

Do you sometimes have an idea that comes to mind, and as hard as you try to push it back into the recesses of your brain it keeps coming forward in your thoughts? *Well, all right, then. If I'm going to write a book, I have to be me: the mother—and the writer—who shares everyday experiences way too often; totally guilty of TMI, always the one to tell on myself first to avoid someone else guessing.* I wanted my book to have humor because my family was spawned in a vat of laughs. But could it be profound and impactful, too? I also wanted to weave in the flair and writing style of Lenore, which is sarcastic, snarky, cynical, yet funny in a kind and loving sort of way.

Free-Range Kids touches on the burdens today's world puts on mothers. The term *free-range* refers to animals that are allowed to roam about their habitat rather than being confined to an enclosure all day long. But when you talk about children being free-range, the idea makes you stop and think about what that really means.

In her book Lenore discusses how being a mother or parent is a position that she believes should not be applauded and revered. In other generations being a parent was just a given role and not a "profession." In my humble opinion, the very idea that parenting is a career that compares to the kind you are hired to do started the whole competition between having the mommy career and the need to be respected as, for example, a *New York Times* journalist. Therefore if we both have careers, yours in a high-rise, mine in a bathroom, then I must rise to the top of my profession and be a better mother than you. How am I going to get my accolades if I'm just an average mom? I have to be the best mom, or the mom who does everything, is perfectly groomed, and makes, dare I say it, homemade things—the mom who must be with her kids 24/7 to keep them safe. Otherwise, back to the mail room for me. No offer of partnership. My name will not be listed on the entryway door—Steelman, Steelman, Steelman, and that loser!

In our children's schools, bullying is a huge topic. Entire assemblies are given on the subject. Children raise their right hand and pledge to honor, respect, and treat each other with kindness. But mean girls still exist and mean girls grow up to be mean moms. The bullying that happens online is incredible.

The revered-mom icon is taken to a whole different level. One of my favorite talks of all time was given by Julie Beck at October Conference 2007. Her talk, "Mothers Who Know," left a lasting impression on me. The first thing she said was:

> The responsibility mothers have today has never required more vigilance. More than at any time in the history of the world, we need mothers who know. Children are being born into a world where they "wrestle not against flesh and blood, but against principalities, against powers, against the rulers of the darkness of this world, against spiritual wickedness in high places." (Ephesians 6:12) However, mothers need not fear. When mothers know who they are and who God is and have made covenants with Him, they will have great power and influence for good on their children.
> (ps://www.lds.org/general-conference/2007/10/mothers-who-know?lang=eng)

Do you know who you are, and are you comfortable just being you? Let's talk about Pinterest, the app from Satan where your food, drink, clothes, home decor, wedding, funeral, and everything else that happens in life must be copied and demonstrated before being authorized. Your child can no longer have a plain old birthday cake in a 9x13-inch pan decorated with frosting marks left by a knife. Your child's first birthday must be celebrated at the museum with a *Tyrannosaurus rex* cake that stands twelve inches tall on its own two feet!

Public shame is rampant these days with social media sites such as Facebook and Twitter, where you can say anything you want. Let me explain how this used to work in the days before Facebook: Gossip was whispered in a confined space. We talked about you, you talked about me, we felt guilty, we went home, repented, brought you a loaf of bread, and offered to watch your kids for the afternoon, secretly thinking that would give you time to clean your house. Then we repented again. It was bad but it was confined badness.

One day my daughter talked about feeling badly that she wasn't playing with her children. I said, "Let's go back and watch *Little House on the Prairie* and see how many times Caroline Ingalls was sitting at the table coloring with Laura or up in the loft playing dolls with Mary. Caroline was working. She was doing laundry. She was cooking. She was farming. She was doing whatever she needed to do. And those kids were gone, playing out on the prairie—all by themselves!" Where did the idea emerge that mothers should not only care for children and home but also entertain children at all times and literally fulfill all the roles needed to help a child grow into a contributing member of society?

I know we live in a different, scary world now. Children in days gone by fell in wells, drowned in lakes, lost limbs from farm equipment. Parents had worries, but they didn't have a box in the house that filled the home with pornography, violence, and vulgarity.

It is a more violent world and no one wants to say, "If only I would have…". But a playground is still a playground and moms should still be allowed to read a book, even if it's on a smart phone, while junior plays by himself. The phrase "helicopter parent," came about in the late 1960s when a book referenced a case study of a teenager who said, "Mother hovers over me like a helicopter…" [Dr. Haim Ginott (1969), *Between Parent and Teenager*, p. 18, New York, NY: Scribner. ISBN 0-02-543350-4.]

The practice of "helicoptering" by parents was born out of fear. You may have heard about the Adam Walsh case of the early 1980s; his father, John Walsh, had the famous and long-running television show, *America's Most Wanted*. Parents all over the country became afraid that if they weren't standing constant watch, something terrible would happen to their child as it had when Adam was kidnapped and murdered. Soon faces of missing children were featured on milk cartons in hopes they would be found safely and returned home.

Terrible things happen, and we have to use common sense and we have to be forgiving to ourselves and to other parents. Why can't I drop off clothes at the cleaners and leave my brood in the car for five minutes? Who decided this was bad parenting? We accepted an alarming event as the norm and concluded that we have complete control over all events in life. But some events are simply out of our control.

If your child is involved in an organized function, you feel you must be sitting there on the sidelines watching them because, heaven forbid, the other parents will notice you're not there and say, "Where is so-and-so's mother? Why isn't she here watching her child? Strip her of her ribbons immediately—no soccer-mom badge for her!"

How can your children learn and grow if they aren't allowed to have the freedom to make mistakes? How can *you*? Let me once again share an example of how I learned not to judge so harshly. When I was pregnant with my first child, we were living in an apartment in Portland, Oregon. There was a lady who lived below us who had one little boy. I would hear her yelling at that little boy through the walls. If I was going down the stairs while she was getting in her car, I could hear her yelling. I remember thinking, "Oh, that poor little boy, that poor little boy."

But then I had my own little boy—a little boy who never walked. He ran. He climbed. He explored. He opened cupboards and climbed on counters. He broke toys to see what was inside. He was independent, curious, and active, and destructive and determined.

My second child was obedient to a fault. He literally stopped sucking his thumb immediately when I suggested he should stop! I cursed the day I explained to him that taking a bottle to bed was not a good idea. He agreed… at eighteen months. When I tried to give one to him anyway that night, he refused. Not taking a bottle was clearly stated in the contract; sleeping was never addressed.

One winter day when I had these two night-and-day different boys and a brand new baby girl, my oldest was nowhere to be found in our tiny two-bedroom apartment. Where could he have gone? I had a hunch. I instantly knew he had let himself out and had gone to the park up the block. I was well aware of his M.O. What do I do? How do I leave my eighteen-month-old and my brand new baby to find this three-year-old boy?"

Because it was a long time ago, I really can't remember whether I walked down to the park or he just came back on his own. But he had decided he wanted to play at the park, so he went down to the park and played, and then he came home. Thank heavens we didn't have the parent police or social media back then that we have today, or I would have been arrested for child neglect and had all of my kids taken away. I could perhaps have negotiated a deal for the three-year-old, but who knows?

You, as a mother, do the best that you can at the time. I bet if you spoke with other young mothers you'd hear similar stories—that is, if they are brave enough to share—or unlucky enough to end up on the local news yet lucky enough that the reporter can say, "No charges have been filed in the incident."

I think we set impossible standards for ourselves and other young women. Any woman dreads the judgment of other women. And it doesn't matter what the subject is!

For instance, I had the house all decorated for Halloween, my favorite holiday. A friend was over, and she kept asking, "Did you make that? Did you make that? Did you make that?" pointing to everything resembling Halloween decorations in the room. In response to each inquiry I said, "No, I bought it. No, I bought it. No, I bought it!" I don't craft. I don't like to craft. I don't like to sew. I don't like to do anything that demands large amounts of time sitting. But I shop at craft shows regularly. I respect that another woman made decorations I can use. I buy the handiwork from her and still feel really good about myself. Later that day my friend posted on Facebook that she didn't have any respect for people who just go out and buy their holiday decorations. She was posting about me!!

Families that have to deal with a challenged child, whether it's a physical, social, or learning disability, find that the "I'm-a-better-mother-than-you" syndrome is compounded. With one in every sixty-eight children being born with autism, there is an entire community of women who have to deal with the additional judgment as to what kind of parent of a *disabled* child they are.

"Have you really searched out every possible therapist? Have you taken your child to every possible therapy and evaluation you could find? Or have you just accepted that your child is that way and that whatever happens, happens?" Once again, guilty as charged.

Years ago I found out that one of the families I saw every week at church had a handicapped child whom they had never brought to church. "What do you mean they don't bring this child to church? Who do they leave her with? If I have to bring *my* handicapped child to church, they should too!" (I'm not sure who I thought told me I had to.) I later learned that the child was very loud and uncontrollable. Secretly I was jealous. I hadn't known it was okay to leave a handicapped child at home. I hadn't known it was okay to go to church as a family and still feel the spirit, participate in the sacrament, and learn in class while TJ was at home. I was so used to standing in the hall and wrangling the other five, I thought his disabilities were just another trial I was expected to deal with!

When TJ was younger I could still carry him, and his wheelchair was tiny and cute. He was tiny and cute. Now he's older, he's bigger, he's louder. He suffers with gastric reflux. We tilt his wheelchair back just enough to prevent him from drooling. Often he concentrates so intently on listening that the saliva puddles in the back of his throat. Then he chokes, and then he coughs. Of course he often does this during the quietest moment of the service. His cough is disturbing and startling. Everybody turns to stare. I put my hand over his mouth and grab a rag to muffle the sound. People are jolted out of their silent prayers and heads turn to make sure he's okay— they love him, they accept him.

I am now that mother from days gone by whom I judged for not bringing her child to church. My child is too loud. I don't like the attention he brings. He will soon be thirty years old. I have done my time. My sentence of experiencing church from the hallways has been fulfilled. I want to sit in the pews with all the other empty-nesters and actually listen to a sermon!

I'm a woman just as you are—a woman who loves her family and has survived many trials. You may be young, you may be my age, or older. You may have children, you may be single. Whatever has happened in your life, whatever your struggles have been, you must be strong for the days ahead. Julie Beck reminds us, "Who will prepare this righteous generation of sons and daughters? Latter-Day Saint women will do this—women who know and love the Lord and bear testimony of Him, women who are strong and immovable and who do not give up during difficult and discouraging times."

I love the message from Eliza R. Snow, the second General Relief Society president, a strong woman who endured many hardships:

> Women should be women and not babies that need petting and correction all the time. I know we like to be appreciated but if we do not get all the appreciation which we think is our due, what matters? We know the Lord has laid high responsibility upon us, and there is not a wish or desire that the Lord has implanted in our hearts in righteousness but will be realized, and the greatest good we can do to ourselves and each other is to refine and cultivate ourselves in everything that is good and ennobling to qualify us for those responsibilities.
> (https://www.lds.org/general-conference/2010/04/and-upon-the-handmaids-in-those-days-will-i-pour-out-my-spirit?lang=eng)

We must regain our strength to be able to achieve everything we have been asked to achieve while on this earth, independent from our husbands, regardless of our situation, and in spite of our struggles. There is a solution, and it comes from Heavenly Father, through us, the mothers.

CHAPTER 9

Strong Women Wanted

In today's world, you need to be a strong woman. The problems you may face—whether financial worries, marriage difficulties, or children with learning, social, or physical disabilities or limitations—are, in their own right, challenging to handle.

You not only need to be able to stand in your trials, but to also stand up, hold your head high, and find the strength to continue each day while going through those challenges. Because after all, living an independent and self-reliant life is admirable, necessary, and part of the American spirit.

But what if you are having trouble seeing your way out of desperation, dealing with a deep sadness or depression, or feeling dependent and needing the assistance of others to survive? Do you then become a burden on the community, a hindrance to progression, or a strain on the kindness and generosity of willing good Samaritans? No. Of course not.

You may have been raised, as I was, to think for yourself and find solutions to problems encountered on your own. Learning to find answers came, perhaps, from being brushed aside by your mother. If she was busy, you might have heard, "Go figure it out for yourself; you'll be just fine."

I remember hearing the modern-day philosopher Byron Katie sharing how, while using her self-reliance and independence, she pulled herself up out of depression and anxiety. Being able to climb out of the darkness under your own resourcefulness is certainly admirable. But while that trait is good to have, it also brings about a certain cynicism regarding helping others in need: "Why are you coming to me for help? What have you done to help yourself? Are you sure you can't help yourself?"

And yet the ability to look at those around you, outside of your own trials, who might be experiencing more dire circumstances than you are, may just be the answer in reaching the resolution necessary to surpass and alleviate your pain and disappointment in the situation.

Every problem, every trial, brings about a solution. At times the answer may not be readily known, but it does appear. Caring for TJ seems eternal. His care is physical more than emotional. In many ways he is easy to care for even though to others it might seem daunting. I began doing for him what any mother does for her infant; I just never stopped. It's become routine and not a break from my normal. I view his care and tending to his every need as far less demanding than what other mothers have to put up with. You may be one of them. And that is what I found when I looked outside myself and my trial with TJ: other people and families have problems much bigger than mine, or ones that I would not want to deal with.

We have been taught the purpose of life, why we are here, where we came from, where we are going. It's not the unknown that begs the "why," but rather the "really?" that we explain. We are perplexed by the enormity of the "why we are here"!

Oscar Wilde is noted as saying, "To live is the rarest thing in the world. Most people exist, that is all." What is considered a good life for some would be torture for another. What is a tortured existence to the outside world may be heaven for those living it.

I think that with the blessings of the understanding the Gospel brings, you gain strength because you're told there is a purpose. There is a plan. There is order. We now have the Proclamation to the World that explains even further what our roles are, and we gain comfort in knowing "I'm a woman, you're a man, I'm a mother, you're a father." Everyone understands they have a role to fulfill. You are a daughter of God—you are special, you are unique, and you can glean strength from that fact.

We all have struggles and challenges. Life is hard. But when we reach out to help another mother or another human being, the effects of our challenges, struggles, and trials are softened a bit and become much more palatable.

My hope and intention are to build your confidence and self-reliance through awareness and gratitude. Pain is not unique; sorrow is not surprising—they're part of the plan. Believe it or not, they're part of the path to happiness.

You are not alone in this life. Many surround you. Many travel beside you. Many other mothers have walked the same path—perhaps with different obstacles along the way, but they were there, nonetheless. You are not alone in your trials.

The women who have gone before you were able to be strong and survived their hard knocks because of the women who had gone before them. One day you, too, will be one of those women. You will become the beacon of light for those who walk with you or watch you from a distance, witnessing the straightness of your back as you walk, your head held high, and the confidence you carry in your stride.

I had no role model to mentor me in my struggles with TJ. My mother is from a family of eight children, no disabilities. I have many cousins, no disabilities. But I had good mothers to watch. My own, of course, and my four aunts who love me as much as my own mother does. I learned how to mother and I am mothering my disabled child the same way I did the other five. I am just doing it for a longer time.

The great poet Robert Frost once said, "In three words I can sum up everything I've learned about life: it goes on." The trials of today become the lessons learned of tomorrow. And they are to be shared. I can share my portion of the disabled world. Your challenges are totally unique to you. I'm sure, however, that many of our times of trial, and those of complete joy, echo each other. We are more alike than different.

The pitfalls of life I have experienced have opened my eyes enough to know I am not in charge. But the determination to go about life using my abilities and being that strong woman, and trying not to create a burden on my community, actually prevented me from hearing the quiet whisper telling me to help women and mothers, maybe like you. I created burdens that were too overwhelming for one person. I rejected the option to yoke myself to someone and share the work. My self-inflicted burdens prevented me from being a tool in the hands of God to lighten the load for someone such as you.

By learning from your past, you progress to your future. You can begin to listen more to that quiet voice; heighten the awareness of hearing a pin drop—being startled at its ting; and recognize the sound of the bugle calling you to action.

I am an eternal optimist, a problem-solver, and a product of my Scottish heritage and my Midwestern upbringing. I believe you must accept your whole self and your life as it is being unfolded, with a grateful heart and a realistic vision.

To have sorrow in your life is to know what real joy is. I share my experiences to inspire you to live your life with a grateful heart and a strong determination. I will cry with you, laugh with you, and learn from you. I have a strong belief in the Gospel of Jesus Christ and believe that sorrow is a gift to enable all to recognize joy.

I also hope you will be able to come to the understanding that you have been placed on this earth to lift up not only yourself, but another who is feeling anguish, sorrow, or hopelessness. In the text and music of Hymn 223 by Will L. Thompson, he says, "Have I done any good in the world today? Have I helped anyone in need? Have I cheered up the sad? Made someone feel glad? If not, I have failed in deed."

You have your own choices, and have the free will to make them. At one time I wanted a career as an interior designer. Yet I realized I would never be a successful interior designer because it was my choice to put my family first. If I were with a client and received a call from a loved one who needed me, I would drop everything to be with them. My true passion is my family, and that's where my love is. They are my priority. I want to be there to care for my family. And that's what I do. It is the choice I made, the choice I make still. But truly, I thought those choices had an expiration date. I thought I would fulfill my role as mother and grandmother, and then someday my husband and I would return to being a couple. We would travel, serve a mission, take advantage of our golden years. I didn't anticipate caring for an adult child until my back gives out or my eyesight fails. Yet I will gladly do so, for the love that TJ's brought to my life makes it all worthwhile.

No matter what choice you've made for your life, if you love what you choose, then know what you are doing is okay. You've made the choice. You don't need anyone's permission—or their misplaced guilt—to do what you love to do. That's why there is free agency, which is a gift from God.

Children are gifts from God. They might come in perfectly shaped bodies or they might come with additional challenges like TJ's. I believe that when he was in my womb, God said, *"Oh, crud! This baby is not forming correctly. His body will be troubled. But his mind is perfect. I will whisper comfort in his ear and instructions in his mother's, and if she listens she will feel his love and my love beyond full recognition and more than she has ever known. If she turns to me, I will show her how to walk this path and we will get through this together."*

I believe God can heal TJ's body, yet why would He? There is a purpose to this trial—there will be something that benefits me and anyone whose life TJ touches. Because I was shielded as a child from many trials my family endured, I didn't know that this would be a chapter in my life. My children, however, did witness many struggles as children and siblings, and now they know that life can be full of joy in spite of horrendous forks in the road. My children have endured the death of a spouse, having children with autism and disabilities, and many other struggles that many of you have also lived. The trials are not the labels given to hardships, but rather what we do with what we've been given. Life isn't always perfect on the outside—or on the inside. We make the best of what we can.

Every day we hear the stories—young mothers die, babies die, fathers are critically injured and are no longer able to provide for their families. Divorce, brain tumors, cancer—they are all recorded and logged. Natural disasters, disasters caused by humans, fires, famine, human injustice. "Fund me" websites pop up daily. The amount of bad luck some families experience makes an Edgar Allen Poe novel look like a fairy tale. We are asked daily to contribute to fundraising events for education reform, medical research, or a family in need. Human empathy and kindness is amazing. What people are doing to offer support by giving and donating their time, talent, and money, especially in the USA, is outstanding. That kind of selflessness is what purpose is all about. It is, dare I say, Christ-like—what we are supposed to do. Charity is the greatest commandment of all.

You can never be in the wrong helping those in need and treating all creatures, whether human or animal, with kindness, love, and charity. Once again, Mrs. Lindbergh:

> I do not believe that sheer suffering teaches. If suffering alone taught, all the world would be wise, since everyone suffers. To suffering must be added mourning, understanding, patience, love, openness, and the willingness to remain vulnerable.

CHAPTER 10

Memories, Mess, and Mishaps

Family is so important. They are the "home" we can go back to.

I don't know if every mother has this dilemma, but I never seem to be able to gather all of my chicks under my wings at the same time anymore. Once they have left the nest, there always seems to be someone missing when we gather.

However, this last Saturday I did it! All six of my children gathered for a run called "The Bubble Run," a fantastically fun and whimsical event that has been equated with Willy Wonka's Bubble Room. I was missing one grandchild, but 99.9 percent of my people ran through the colored bubbles with me. The excitement in their faces, the joy in their squeals, and the happiness everyone was feeling was celestial. If "empty nest" is a disease, having your loved ones run through rainbow bubbles is the medicine.

With those warm, summery remembrances comes the humbug of Ebenezer Scrooge, something that has plagued me for about fifteen years. I have wonderful memories of Christmas, and used to worship and adore every cheesy thing about that holiday season.

My first daughter was born on December 3rd, so our tradition was that no decorations went up until after her birthday. We celebrated her sixth birthday with all her little friends at Burger King in Northeast Portland. I was nine months pregnant and hadn't been feeling well. I remember thinking, "Good thing this baby isn't due until December twenty-third." In spite of everything, I was still prepared for Christmas giving.

The flu-like symptoms continued, and I didn't have the energy to tackle the stairs in our 1850s-built home. Laundry was in the basement, bedrooms on the second floor, our bedroom in the attic. When my water broke early on the morning of December 5th, my first thought was, *Oh, crud, I'd better get that laundry done!*

I slowly tried to sneak out of the bed so as not to wake up Tony. I thought I had hours of labor to endure and wanted him to get as much sleep as he could. I raised my head off the pillow, started to swing my legs off the mattress, and felt a "whoosh." I knew my water had broken, but how much water was I retaining? I decided to wake Tony up. He turned on the light, and to our horror we saw the bed was covered in blood.

At the hospital I was in a private room, thankfully, grateful for the privacy. But I was totally alone—no baby, no spouse, no physical being with me. I had instead the company of the true comforter, the only arms that could reach me those few days, the spirit of the Lord.

I have warm memories of carolers strolling the hospital wing singing "Silent Night." I felt close to the Savior, knowing the feeling of having given birth in a situation that was not ideal, knowing this baby's life was in His hands, and knowing that he was a gift and that we were at His mercy.

Like the little drummer boy, young women I had taught at church brought gifts they couldn't afford. Most of them came from families struggling financially and spiritually, and downtrodden with trials of their own.

In contrast to the tender, quiet voice that comforted me in the hospital, a much louder voice rang in my ear after I was released from the hospital. Peace and love gave way to the chaos that the world's idea of Christmas brings.

My distaste for the month of December began when my children got older and present-buying became expensive and tasking. Odds were one of them would be upset on Christmas morning. Gifts that I had searched for, nabbed, and scored were somehow off. I remember sitting downstairs one Yule morning actually yelling, "You kids get down here right now and open gifts!" I'm sure there was a superlative or two added indicating that their very lives were in danger and they had better be happy when they came down those stairs!

I also began to tire of the obligatory family get-together. I wanted to instill our own family traditions but was always forced to attend gatherings that Tony's family had planned. My family still lived in the Midwest, so because of the travel involved, we never had to endure the alternating-year fiasco. I did put my foot down a few times, but the reality was that neither one of my brothers had children, and with the only cousins being on the Steelman side, Christmas Eve with "just us" seemed underwhelming.

So what brought back my spirit of Nativity, my happiness for "the most wonderful time of the year?" You guessed it: GRANDCHILDREN! Babies! Little people gasping with joy when something as simple as a matchbox car is opened. A four-year-old girl who asks a hundred times, "Do I look beautiful in my new nightgown?" A two-year-old who believes that the grandfather who just left the room is indeed the REAL Santa Claus now appearing at the front door.

Christ gathered the little children and said, "Behold, you little ones." Christmas was made for children, and I was reunited with the true meaning of the season through a child, because of a child, for a child.

The turmoil that a mother feels when she has to continue to love a child who doesn't deserve to be loved is indescribable. The other children in the family deserve to be defended, protected, and made a priority, and yet the lost lamb keeps calling you back and you run.

The obedient children can't understand why you continue to put in time and energy for the repeat offender. The prodigal son parable is missing a few chapters; I know for certain there is more to that story! You hate what this love does, you want to quit, and like the Monday-morning diet, you swear this is it. It's heroin for your heart.

On the love scale, brotherly love and a mother's love have no gray—they're black and white. When you've lived long enough to be a sibling AND a mother to adult children, you know and feel that strange emotional bungee ride.

Mothers make lists and count the Christmas gifts under the tree to make sure the children all receive what she perceives to be equal. Children count the gifts and from the age of eight to eighty-eight swear that "Suzie" was spoiled and indulged her whole life because once in 1936 she received *three* gifts and they only got two.

You want your children to achieve equal success, happiness, and your love and attention. Intellectually you know that is never possible, but emotionally mothers are, at this very moment, trying to *make* it happen.

Adult siblings shake their heads and throw up their hands when Mom and Dad rush to aid the child who never reaches the proverbial bottom. The flip side is the sibling who doesn't speak to her parents any longer because she feels they didn't help her sister when her sister needed it the most, and she "had" to step in.

My mother is eighty-three years old, and when she calls to talk about her concerns over my grown adult siblings, my gut reaction is, "They are adults. Why do you still care? Why are you still involved?" Then I talk to her about my adult children and she thinks, "They are adults. Why do you still care? Why don't you let them solve their own problems?" It's fascinating.

I listen as my adult children "counsel" me on how I should stop being so involved in the lives of their siblings. What is the cut-off age? When do mothers legally and lawfully get to quit caring and trying to fix the problems of their children? There are two official dates you can choose. Your choices are 1) when you are dead, and 2) when you fake your death and live out your peaceful, selfish life on an island with meals prepared daily by someone named Henri.

I feel a terminal illness coming on, I hope my passport hasn't expired!

Oh, and let's not forget about how birth order determines your lot in life and just how much of your personality is developed or influenced by it. This subject has been researched and hypothesized to death. In my many "ladies' baby-shower" discussion groups, the subject of our children's personalities range from, "They just came out that way" to "He's just like his father" (which isn't always a compliment) and "How can children raised in the same home be so different?" Not often is their birth order ever discussed. There are so many variables in birth-order theories that even the experts don't agree about them. Are first-born children high achievers and driven due to all the parental attention, or are they spoiled narcissists because of that same dynamic?

The idea that you have typical personality traits depending on your birth order began in 1920 with Alfred Alder, the Austrian psychiatrist. Since then this discussion has gone the way of most "expert" opinions and varies with each decade—giving us just enough time to screw up one generation.

My expert opinion, one that I value highly above others, is that you get it all. If I had to choose which firstborn I'd like to say I mothered, it would be Oprah. Some examples of last-born children are Steve Martin and Rosie O'Donnell.

I do, however, see similar personalities in middle children. I have an aunt who, in her eighties, still harbored resentment for the lack of attention she received because she was in the middle of eight children. My own little middle is just now finding out that in spite of not having a baby book and few pictures of her as a newborn, she was loved and dearly wanted.

Then there is the "devil/angel" theory. This is when one child becomes "the Beaver" because the other child is "Eddie Haskell." (For you younger readers, *Leave It to Beaver* was a television show from the fifties and sixties with the well-intentioned "Beaver" and the ever-conniving Eddie Haskell.) Let me tell you about my "Beaver."

I got out his baby book. Yes, the first two kids had them, but only, thank the heavens, because there wasn't this insane scrapbooking craze back in 1978. Mothers my age remember the days when you stuck a little piece of hair on a non-biodegradable page with good-old yellowing Scotch Tape, wrote "first haircut" with a plain old Bic pen, and felt good about it.

By the way, sidebar here, I also remind my middle child that I didn't swear until she came along. Sorry, but when you have surpassed the number of your hands in the number of children you have, verbal outbursts are not always prayers.

Back to my angel child: I was reading in his book that he was such a good baby. I wrote, "He slept all night the first night and has ever since." Doesn't that just make you sick? I then wrote, "He has only had one night that he didn't go to sleep until two a.m. Besides that he usually goes to sleep at ten-thirty and sleeps until six, I feed him, and he goes back to sleep until eight."

In his book is recorded his first talk that he gave in Primary at the age of three. He recited a poem that he memorized:

A bunch of golden keys are mine, to make each day with gladness shine.
"Good morning" is the golden key that unlocks every door for me.

The poem goes on for three more verses. My little star received a standing ovation! The Primary president asked, "How did you do that?" Oh yeah, that was a proud moment.

When this child was in the seventh grade, we attended his teacher conference. The teacher began by telling us there was another "Steelman" in the school (his older brother). "Are they related?" he asked.

"Yes, that is his older brother," we replied.

The teacher paused, then paused again. Then he asked, "From the same marriage?"

Now, what does that say about nature versus nurture? Our second son never ran with a crowd. He always had one friend—one really good friend. Change was hard for him because he was shy, and the thought of moving away from his one friend at any given time was unbearable for him. Once we moved from three acres in the country to the "burbs," and he was devastated. But soon he made friends with a great young man his age from our church. His one friend had been replaced with a new "one friend." When he entered middle school and high school, his one-friend rule expanded, and he had a little gang in no time—friends from work, friends from FBL, friends from band.

I noticed then that school counselors are like parents; they only have time for the kids who are exceptionally brilliant or terribly disturbed. The students who don't make any waves are brushed aside. When meeting with them about some trouble our oldest son was having, I would mention son #2 and they would shuffle papers and look at computer screens in confusion. "There is another Steelman at this school?"

When it came time for college, there wasn't a question where son #2 would go. He was going where his friends were headed, Oregon State. Any family that holds tight to religious beliefs, whether it be Catholic, Jewish, Muslim, or Mormon, is devastated when members of the family start to wander in another direction. We wanted him to attend Brigham Young University (BYU), but going to a school by himself was out of the question for him.

We trusted that he would continue attending church while at Oregon State, but by his second year we felt it necessary to give him an ultimatum: either start attending church, go to BYU, or pay for college on his own. We thought we were doing the tough love thing. We envisioned him bearing his testimony, accepting that this challenge changed his life, and being thankful for our intervention. However, not only did he lose valuable credits by transferring to BYU, his resentment overpowered any chance of the spirit touching him, though he followed the university rules, attended all the religion classes required, and even participated in a volunteer calling within the congregation.

That darn free agency thing! The young men of the church are encouraged to go on a mission when they turn eighteen. None of our eligible sons chose that route, and when one of them returned to church activities after being away from them, he admitted that not having served a mission can make reentry difficult. I admit that serving a mission is kind of a given, and when men gather, the conversation is often wrapped around their missions: "Where did you go? Who was your favorite companion?" It's the proverbial boys' club. They slap backs and reminisce over wrecked bikes and dog bites.

As a mother attending services regularly, when other young men would announce their mission call or give their farewell talk, it hit the gut. Tears were shed; I had feelings of inadequacy. These feelings were the same ones I had when it took me a full year to get pregnant and I watched babies being blessed, not having one of my own to be blessed.

One day it hit me. I was sobbing behind the wheel of my car. After all, that is the best place to sob and to totally pull a "poor me" attitude. Really, isn't that what inadequacy is? It's all about you; it's all about me. Inadequacy is a very selfish emotion. Who makes you inadequate? No one but YOU! How do you, yourself, feel inadequate? By comparing your success to someone else's success, that's how. It's a form of coveting. "I coveted your son's mission."

The Spirit burst through my selfish sobs and yelled, "Cut it out! What is the matter with you? This isn't about you. This is what free agency is all about." I realized then and there that I was blessed with truly amazing sons—hardworking and very kind. They keep our family in stitches, and a vacation isn't a vacation if one of them isn't there. College memories and childhood pranks are retold with such love. What the heck was I crying about? Talk about being ungrateful.

From that point on I never felt a twinge of sorrow when I attended mission farewells. Our oldest daughter did choose to serve mission, and our home was so blessed by her devotion. But her mission was for her, and those she served, not us. She served and we received collateral blessings. It was her free agency and not anything about us. We are so proud of this choice of course, but recognize it as her life's journey. In the Sermon on the Mount we read, "And why beholdest thou the mote that is in thy brother's eye, but considerest not the beam that is in thine own eye?"

I've got a lumber yard in my eye that it is going to take a literal lifetime to work. In Jacob 4:3 we read concerning the scriptures, "hoping that our beloved brethren and our children will receive them with thankful hearts, and look upon them what they may learn with joy and not with sorrow, neither with contempt, concerning their first parents."

I am so grateful for free agency, and continue to pray that our children will see the joy that religion and scriptures have brought us, not the sorrow.

CHAPTER 11

How Long, Lord?

"Come to Me, all who are weary and heavy-laden, and I will give you rest. Take My yoke upon you and learn from Me, for I am gentle and humble in heart, and you will find rest for your souls."

—*Matthew 11:28-29*

You may feel that your marriage is being challenged by disharmony in your home, or your faith is being tested because you feel that your prayers are not being answered or are going unheard. Or you may feel that nothing has ever brought you to the point where you couldn't do something by yourself. You've never felt the need for a yoke or to be lifted up. Me too! I've always held the belief that I can do whatever "this" is.

If you are like me, you have the Gospel. You have a testimony. You have faith. With all these resources, you expect that you'll be just fine. You know God is helping every step of the way. You just have never felt you couldn't do something alone... and that you could do everything. You are the "all right, let's fix this, let's see what we need to do" independent type of woman: "I've got this."

But too much of life can happen all at once. For instance, my husband just retired. The time has finally arrived that most in this country work for—those golden years. We were looking forward to a life of leisure, of traveling to distant places and enjoying our grandchildren. This time in life should be a happy one when we return to being a couple. I thought I could retire from day-to-day mothering duties at this time, too. Yet, and with total transparency, in meeting both my son's and my grandson's needs, some days I think I've finally reached my limit. I'm not certain I can—or want to—"be all and do all" anymore. Those retirement dreams of travel and adventure may not happen as easily, or at all, as I once thought.

I'm at the point where I don't know what the future is or holds, nor do I know how everything is going to work out. I think everything that is happening right now and that will occur in the future will be really hard. Somedays I lose hope. I'm going to need a lot of support from up high, and the journey is certainly going to be interesting.

Reality has a way of bringing you to your knees. Loss of hope is not only a sign of being discouraged, but also signals depression. I wish people would talk about this topic more than they do. The cause of depression can be a chemical imbalance, but what if your depression is caused by an outside influence and not just by feelings internally felt from the experience?

Some people would honestly look at my life and say, "She has everything." Yet they might also recognize the depression, and therefore say, "I don't blame her for losing hope; she's got a lot going on right now."

Depression can come from hoping for things that do not become reality, such as children, more children, a great career, glowing good health, or an easy life. Then there are employment issues, health crises, natural disasters, or—the worst—a loss suffered because of someone else's failure to follow laws or their mental illness. You can come to the conclusion that a situation has caused your shortcomings or failure to follow the commandments, or that something is lacking in your nature. Perhaps you feel unworthy, which caused prayers to not be answered.

This feeling of lost hope or depression is not what I had planned for my life or the lives of my children. Have you ever felt this way?

In Luke 8:43 we read of a woman who had a blood disease and had faith that Jesus could heal her. This account has been taught to students and to believers in the power of prayer and that faith in Jesus Christ will heal our hearts and our bodies. The story reminds us to have perfect faith and that Christ's blessings require small acts on our part with great abundance of love from Christ.

I got a new view of this familiar Bible story from S. Michael Wilcox, the recently retired instructor of the Institute of Religion at the University of Utah. Dr. Wilcox gave a talk entitled "The Jesus We Need to Know." In his lesson he opened my eyes to the truth behind this woman's dilemma and desperation. He explained that in biblical days, if you had a blood issue as she did, the law of Moses, as described in the book of Leviticus, required that no one touch you, ever. Even if you were to sit upon something, that seat could not be touched. If anyone did touch you, they would be considered unclean. This biblical woman was an unclean outcast, all because of illness.

The woman's faith gave her the knowledge that if only Jesus could touch her, she would be healed. But her compassion for others and for Jesus kept her from asking him for this blessing. She did not want to burden him or condemn him to this life that she endured. She thought, "Maybe if I just touch the hem of his garment, lightly and innocently, he won't know that I touched him, and therefore he cannot be held responsible for this act. He will not be condemned to being unclean like me."

The woman desperately touched one finger to the bottom of Jesus's robe—just enough to capture his power and grace. She was healed. Her joy was brief, however, as it was instantly changed to fear when Jesus turned and asked, "Who touched me?" I love how his disciples responded as if to almost sarcastically say, "Really? We are surrounded by thousands of people and you ask who just brushed against you?"

Jesus continued, however, and explained that this was not just a brush. He had felt virtue move from him. The meaning of the word *virtue* is "power." He felt some of his priesthood power leave his body as if he had just blessed someone, and yet he hadn't.

When the woman saw that Jesus knew someone had touched him, she was afraid. She was afraid that she would be condemned for her sin, for her breaking of the law. She thought she would hide, but when their eyes met, she saw that she could not hide from his all-knowing eyes, and she began to tremble. She thought she had committed a sin that could not be forgiven, and that she had also caused another to be condemned.

Jesus looked upon her with love and tenderness, comforted and acknowledged her, and said, "Daughter, be of good comfort: thy faith hath made thee whole; go in peace."

You may fear and tremble over your sins and unworthiness as a mother and a daughter of God. However, the daughter of God mentioned in Luke had faith she would be healed and she was. Why can't prayers, temple, and church attendance be enough to change hearts as quickly as this woman had been healed?

This is where life has caught up with me. I don't wish to resent anyone for the joys and happiness they have; I want to appreciate the blessing parts of this life and not die with a bitter heart. Brother Wilcox's wise words augmented my knowledge of what faith really means: *Faith is to hope for things which are not seen, but which are true.*

My Bible dictionary explains, "…miracles do not produce faith but strong faith is developed by obedience to the Gospel of Jesus Christ; in other words, faith comes by righteousness, although miracles often confirm one's faith." Faith cannot be based on untruths. It is a principle of action. We must do all that we can to fulfill our own destiny. A lack of faith can lead one to despair.

EUREKA! The light bulb shines brightly! The depression which I have been feeling, the lack of faith I have, is my own doing! Joy is found in faith that Christ heals all in His own ways and time.

Blessings are to be recognized, and thankfulness can bring the joy that helps pull you out of the depths of despair—also known as the world we must live in.

In regard to the despair I felt over unfulfilled dreams, it was once again made known to me that 1) either my dreams were not mine to dream, or 2) my truth is not my truth, but rather based on the world's standards of what truth is.

It is not meant for all daughters of God to live the same life on this earth. We are each blessed with our own destiny, our own path, our own story. The only thing we have in common is our duty to follow the commandments of God; to find out for ourselves who we are, what we are, and where we want to end.

"I am a Child of God. He has sent me here, has given me an earthly home. Lead me, guide me, walk beside me, help me find the way. Teach me all that I must do, to live with him someday."
—from the song "I am a child of God" by Naomi W. Randall

Solution Panic

However, and even with the joy of that new revelation, you may be feeling once again the depression felt before. You are praying more, yet you may also be crying more. You're not only looking for a solution, you are *panicked* about finding one. Plus you are a little afraid. I know how you feel.

In order to help with our new challenge of raising our grandson, who will soon be struggling with his challenges as a teenager, I listened to a TED Talk given by a girl who has autism spectrum disorder (ASD), a developmental disorder affecting the ability to effectively socialize and communicate. To hear her say she's gone through eleven different therapies and medications frightens me. We've already been through four doctors trying to get help for our grandson, and I'm afraid of what's next. I'm afraid that life with this little guy is not going to be as easy as the other "life" I have with TJ.

Life is easy with TJ because I've had thirty years to create a routine that works.

It's not that I don't have experience with kids who struggle. I raised his father, after all! In my head, however, I hear the words of Frank Sinatra: "When I was seventeen, it was a very good year..." Let's be honest; I was younger when I had boys in junior high and I was not as wise to the fact that you can do everything right and things can still go so very wrong.

I'm in panic mode to find a solution to help not only myself with this added responsibility, but more so to find the help my grandson needs. I am blessed to have a car and medical insurance to cover the costs of his care. And when I reflect on how hard it is for me to help him, I begin to think about what it's like for single mothers who must deal with their children all by themselves, or for the family whose father has lost his job and the medical insurance with it. The first thing medical facilities want to know when you call to set up an appointment is the name of your insurance carrier. How do those families cope?

You may be not only at the bottom of the pit, wondering and worrying about what you will do next to survive and get through the day, but also in another, better place of empathy and sympathy. The roadblocks, hurdles, and obstacles you run up against bring recognition and awareness that you are not the only one suffering with or experiencing these drastic episodes. You are now able to look outside of your own trials to be supportive, sharing the knowledge you've gained with those who walk beside you in this journey of life. The path, however, is not easy, and remains filled with challenges that demand, threaten, and test your strength and faith.

I thought my mothering challenge was going to be completed in twenty-six years. I had in my head that TJ was going to die when he was twenty-six years old, and therefore I had a 9,490-day challenge. Someone once casually mentioned to me that they had a friend with a child who had cerebral palsy who died when he was twenty-six. That is where I got that crazy idea!

When the twenty-six years were over, I realized he wasn't going to die and I would have to take care of TJ for the rest of my life. *But I didn't sign up for this long challenge.* Now, before you get all uptight with the previous sentence, let me say right here and now that wanting someone to die is not a very politically correct thing to admit to. I believe, however, that it is human to want pain or injustice to stop.

I watch TJ scrunch up his eyes and wrinkle his nose and not be able to scratch an itch. I check his body every night and watch for hot spots where the skin is breaking down because of sitting in his wheelchair all day. I've watched his face pale and listened to him cry because of some illness or pain that he can't tell me about, and I can only guess how to help him. I've seen his suffering and I pray daily for him to be released from this wretched body he was given. He is my life, but it's just human to want to have closure or an end to a challenge. I want him to have the joy of going to Heavenly Father and having a perfect body. You may be shocked, but a mother's love means always wanting what is best for her child. I will care for TJ with love and tenderness for as long as he lives, but will rejoice the day he completes his mission here on earth and goes to paradise. He deserves it.

I always wonder about the "30-day challenge" or the "28-day challenge" to be smarter, thinner, or richer. After thirty days, then what? Will you go back to where you were before starting the personal contest? Life is not a 28- or 30-day challenge. *Life is forever.*

While there are programs out there that are beneficial and can change the mindset necessary to succeed, most of these challenges or contests just set you up for more disappointment at the end of those twenty-eight or thirty days. When the challenge is over and you've made it through without ingesting sugar, processed food, or dairy products, chances are the celebration and reward of that success will be to grab a donut and swing through Burger King.

An expectation that a challenge will be over soon, whether it is dropping ten pounds before my class reunion or expecting TJ to live only until twenty-six, can be a problem, especially when you're expecting a certain outcome. Your expectations can become a source of disappointment and despair.

Quit making life a game. Stop marking your calendar when you think your challenge is going to be over. Just accept life the way it is and just do it. Just do life—because there is a good possibility something else is going to come your way. That's life! (I hear another Frank Sinatra song.)

While it may be true that I have no good news to share with you, here is where I go back to the "why" of writing this book. It is not my intention to depress or scare you, but rather to help lift the burden you may be experiencing. Look all around for the silver lining of what you're experiencing. Notice what you do have—even the smallest of possessions that help you through each day.

You may become aware that your trials are far easier than what your neighbor has to deal with. As the saying goes, "If we hung our burdens on the line, you'd take yours and I'd take mine!" You may not have a handicapped or socially-challenged child, but I wouldn't want your woes. I'll take my own, thank you very much! That is the silver lining.

CHAPTER 12

Remember Who You Are

Erma Bombeck had it right in *The Grass is Always Greener over the Septic Tank.* Before you get that nice carpet of green to grow, a lot of fertilizer needs to be put down first.

Your grass may not be as green as your neighbor's, but it's your grass, darn it! You might not really want that green grass, anyway, because once you realize how much work it takes to maintain it, you just might be good with a half-brown, half-green lawn. There is no rule that you must keep up with the Joneses, the Smiths, or the neighbor who hires a company to service their lawn. If you feel satisfied you've done the best you can at the moment, being focused on more important issues such as your family, then you are in the spot, the very place, where you need to be.

Although I relate to Ms. Bombeck and love her humor, one of my favorite books is written by Jeannette Walls: *The Glass Castle.* It's a true account of her young life and situations she didn't make for herself. What that woman went through in the 1980s with her artistic parents, homelessness, living in the Ozarks, starving, snow coming through the roof—you would think her tale happened one hundred twenty-five years ago, and not merely twenty-five years ago.

In her book Walls describes how one day while taking a sociology class, the discussion revolved around the homeless. She raised her hand and said, "You know, sometimes, we just have to admit these people are homeless because they want to be." Walls admitted later that she received a firm scolding from her professor and other members of the class for that comment. She did not divulge to the class, however, that that was her reality; that her parents had chosen the homeless life.

Sometimes we do create our own problems. Realizing you have a self-inflicted problem doesn't mean you're a bad person or that there is no chance for redemption. The first step to correcting your path is to acknowledge your part in your lot in life. Gazing at your life side by side with what others are experiencing is another way to put perspective on your struggles. It's time to make the situation better.

Let's talk about free agency and being in situations that occur which are not controlled by you. I believe this was the deciding factor when determining the plan of salvation. The late Robert D. Hales reminded us in his talk at the October Conference of 2010, "We teach that agency is the ability and privilege God gives us to choose and 'to act for [ourselves] and not to be acted upon.'" (https://www.lds.org/general-conference/2010/10/agency-essential-to-the-plan-of-life?lang=eng)

Free agency is to act with accountability and responsibility for our actions. It is essential to understand and recognize what this means. With it we are "free to choose liberty and eternal life, through the great Mediator of all men…" (2 Nephi 2:27). I believe that often the gift of free agency creates trials and sadness in our lives through no fault of our own, and not because it was "God's will." For example, if someone used his free agency to drink and drive, and therefore hit my car, causing my death, I don't believe the accident or my death were God's will. When I died, it may not have been my time to leave this earth, but it was God's way of letting the universe go in the way He designed it. I believe he could have intervened and does intervene often, but it isn't always necessary.

President Spencer W. Kimball wrote:

Did our Father in heaven cause the collision of the cars that took six people into eternity, or was it the error of the driver who ignored safety rules?…Could the Lord have prevented these tragedies? The answer is, Yes. The Lord is omnipotent, with all power to control our lives, save us pain, prevent all accidents, drive all planes and cars, feed us, protect us, save us from labor, effort, sickness, even from death, if he will. But he will not. We should be able to understand this, because we can realize how unwise it would be for us to shield our children from all effort, from disappointments, temptations, sorrows, and suffering. (https://www.lds.org/manual/teachings-spencer-w-kimball/chapter-2?lang=eng)

People often use the vile acts of men to claim a disbelief in any God. If there is a God, for example, how can He allow young girls to be sold into slavery in Thailand? You have to step back from the situation a bit to reconcile it. God gives us free agency to do what we will. Many use their free agency to carry out despicable acts against the world for personal gain—circumstances out of our control—maybe.

I believe that the entire world is under God's watchful eye. He sees the atrocities, he is aware of the calamities. As a Christian I believe that God wants all the world to turn to Him, but He will force no one. It must be our choice to love and to appreciate one another.

One problem that occurs when we try to solve the evil actions of men with manly solutions is we usually create another problem. I fear there is a culture today of young people who believe that everyday problems are more acute than they are; that bad things are not meant to fall in their paths and that everyone should help make those problems go away. Online money-raising sites such as Go Fund Me pop up almost before the ink on the prescription is dry.

I can't help but speculate that this thinking is a result of the panic that spread after the 1999 Columbine High School massacre. This horrific act by two young men made many wonder how this could have happened and what we can do to prevent it from happening again. Self-esteem became the buzzword. Children with a feeling of high worth, it was concluded, would never commit such a heinous act.

Shortly after this event, the high school that my children attended demanded that all posters for athletic events cheer the competing side as well as encouraging our team to win. They arranged for an assembly at which any child who had never received an award was recognized for something. Students actually received certificates for attending school five days in a row! A quote from an article in *The Huffington Post* reads, "Perhaps we should start calling those under 25 years old the 'participation trophy generation.'" (https://www.washingtonpost.com/news/the-fix/wp/2014/08/20/meet-the-participation-trophy-generation/)

I see this mindset now in our younger sisters. Being a mother is tough. Raising a family is never-ending stress. There are usually few accolades and never will there be a trophy—just the joy of watching your grown children laugh together about their time as children and thank you after forty years for giving them that gift.

My friend and I were recently discussing the dilemma of offering prayers to heal when someone is sick or disabled. Friends and extended family, perhaps, pray that the person gets better. A few parents, however, pray that their loved one will die and be relieved from the suffering. Has the person lived a good long life and is now frail and alone? Is it a child whose quality of life will be minimal if they survive? Who's to say?

I use TJ as an example. I believe his body didn't form correctly, thereby creating multiple medical issues. I also believe God was a witness to TJ's physical calamity and was saddened that his body was set to betray him. I don't believe He created TJ's body in this fashion or wanted him to endure his time on earth in this way, but He was aware and He knew that lessons would be gained from this experience. He didn't "give" me this trail; He is watching what I am doing with it.

I didn't choose this child; he was given to me. I didn't put on a sash of strength; I just take care of him the way I took care of the other humans who were placed in my care. I have my bad days. I have fallen on my knees and begged for Heavenly Father to take TJ back; to relieve me of this burden. And sometimes I still do. Many mornings I open his bedroom door and hope that he has passed into the next world silently and painlessly during the night. I don't think I am alone in having such thoughts. I am reminded of the scripture Matthew 26:39 that says, "And he went a little further, and fell on his face, and prayed, saying if it be possible, let this cup pass from me; nevertheless not as I will, but as thou wilt." We, too, want our cares and our burdens to be lifted.

We as women are being asked to do more as the years progress. The age for missionary service has been lowered. More women are going out into the world to spread the Gospel than ever before. This takes courage, strength, and independence. No longer can everything be done in a group. You have to make decisions based on your own inspiration and determination. The time has arrived to stand up and start dealing with reality.

I love Elder Dallin H. Oaks's message from October Conference in 2005. He spoke about his mother and how she cared for the family after his father died. He spoke with pride about how his mother was the head of the home, and then he said:

About this same time, we had a neighbor who dominated and sometimes abused his wife. He roared like a lion, and she cowered like a lamb. When they walked to church, she always walked a few steps behind him. That made my mother mad. She was a strong woman who would not accept such domination, and she was angry to see another woman abused in that way. I think of her reaction whenever I see men misusing their authority to gratify their pride or exercise control or compulsion upon their wives in any degree of unrighteousness. (See D&C 121:37.) (https://www.lds.org/general-conference/2005/10/priesthood-authority-in-the-family-and-the-church?lang=eng)

We cannot be women who wither when our husbands aren't home to help us with our role as nurturers. We must be strong enough to be the head of the home if the time ever comes. Professions have changed quickly in the last few decades. In times past, gender roles were more defined and one did not meddle so often in the other's role. I am certainly not advocating we digress fifty years, but some of the good has been thrown out with the bad.

Many men still must leave their homes and travel to support their families. Many women will tell you that there is a cosmic rule that only allows children to become deathly ill when the husband is out of town. Men are no longer a pasture away if something needs done in the home. We cannot become paralyzed as mothers if our partners are not home to assist us on a daily basis.

Our roles have been defined and partners are obligated to assist each other when necessary. We have been given a charge by the First Presidency of The Church of Jesus Christ of Latter-Day Saints. In the Family Proclamation we read:

By divine design, fathers are to preside over their families in love and righteousness and are responsible to provide the necessities of life and protection for their families. Mothers are primarily responsible for the nurture of their children. In these sacred responsibilities, fathers and mothers are obligated to help one another as equal partners. Disability, death, or other circumstances may necessitate individual adaptation. Extended families should lend support when needed.

A few years ago my daughter, who was barely twenty-five at the time, lost her husband in a horrific car accident. She was five months pregnant with their second little girl. Their first daughter was only twenty months old. When she called to deliver the heart-wrenching news and to tell us we needed to come to Seattle to help, she was in shock, but she was stoic and strong. She knew she had to be in charge to get through the next few weeks. She made funeral arrangements. She comforted her distraught father-in-law who had lost his only son. She even made arrangements to meet with the man who had killed her husband to let him know that she forgave him.

Once we had said our final good-byes, laying flowers at his mausoleum that would hold two someday, we packed up her home and took her back to our home where she once again felt like a child and not the responsible wife and mother she was. I heard her sobbing in the quiet of our spare bedroom. She had a baby to deliver soon and another to care for. She was back in her parents' home with no privacy or control over her life. Her birthday was approaching. We all gathered around her physically, but the person who was meant to be her companion was gone. Her life was destroyed in one fatal morning.

She put her daughters' needs before her own. She had to do life in this new way whether she liked it or not. Months passed before she was able to establish a home of her own once again. She continued to have family pictures taken, to visit friends, to attend church and hold a calling. She refused to even consider attending a singles Ward. She had an eternal family and she vowed to live the rest of her life with her daughters.

Heavenly Father had another plan. After many years a young man came into her life and her perspective changed. She knew that her daughters deserved a father on earth. She fell in love again and now is the mother of four.

One never knows where life is going to lead you. Develop your strength. Sharpen the tools used to create the smart, strong woman you know you are. Step up as a leader of and for other women so they can see by example what strength and leadership really is.

Become a mentor. Tell stories of your own failures, trials, and trepidations. Don't be afraid to tell others about your struggles. Perfection gets old, and soon the facade falls. It's okay to admit that being a mother isn't all it's cracked up to be. It's okay to talk about your hard days and to let the dishes sit for days! Who cares? Share stories of the struggles you have with your children. Perfect children do not exist, in spite of the Facebook posts!

There's freedom in being able to be honest and be who you truly are, especially when you find your strength and your voice. You can be kind and respectful, yes, but there are times when you need to just shut situations down. It's okay to be a tough, get-over-yourself kind of person, yet in a loving, understanding, and empathetic way.

Your problems may be much more burdensome than mine—the last thing in the world I want to do is diminish them or you. What I want you to be aware of, however, is that your role as a mother is being challenged more and more each day. In spite of the trend to bear a darling baby bump and parade children like champion pets, the role that you have chosen is still unique. You may be seen as an inspiration to those who watch how you handle the challenges of life that come to you. Remember who you are. Don't lose yourself in the pressure to be all things to all people. The PTA doesn't need you as much as your own children do.

In Alma 56:39 it says, "And they rehearsed unto me the words of their mothers, saying: We do not doubt our mothers knew it."

Do you know who you are, and are you willing to stand alone if need be?

CHAPTER 13

Walkers, Runners, and Wheelers

It was a beautiful Saturday. TJ and I were home alone. Tony was at a business meeting and our grandson was at a camp-out. A fundraiser for United Cerebral Palsy called. "Walk, Roll, or Run" was being held in downtown Portland. I had known about the event days before, but I was hesitant to sign up. I first like to see what kind of day it's going to be weather-wise, and whether getting up at six in the morning to dress TJ will be worth the trip downtown. But when I woke up that Saturday morning I thought to myself, *Yeah, I can to do this.*

Arriving downtown we parked and then registered for the run. There were three different events you could take part in: run a 5K, run an 8K, or do a two-and-a-half-mile walk. I could easily walk the two-and-a-half miles. And if I could run the 5K, I could certainly run the 8K.

Completing my registration for the 8K, I looked around, confused. *Where are all the people with cerebral palsy?* After all, this was the United *Cerebral Palsy* Walk, Roll, or Run fundraiser. Oh sure, there were lots of runners and strollers with babies in them, but there was nobody there—and I mean nobody—who looked handicapped. Well, okay, there was one lady in a wheelchair—who didn't have cerebral palsy—and one girl who looked like she did have cerebral palsy, but that was it.

Some days TJ is just plain not happy, and today was one of them. The few days before the race he had been really fussy, too.

No matter whether he was with me or with Tony on outings—or wherever we were, for that matter—he was fussy. But I'm so used to that. We don't know what's wrong because he can't communicate. So we try to guess. If the fussing and whining stop, we really don't have a clue as to why. His moods come and go, and in waves. Other days he is happy and content. We have learned to take each day as it comes.

All during the run, however, TJ fussed, whined, and was clearly irritated. But the weather was perfect for a run. The race began at nine o'clock, and with the route paved the entire way, we did well and made good time. By ten o'clock I was feeding him and giving him a drink of water.

Then we walked around to all the booths, and suddenly I saw all kinds of people, and many in wheelchairs. I realized that the run had been at nine o'clock, but the two-and-a-half-mile walk was at ten-thirty. I began to pat myself on the back. I was the only person who had a child with cerebral palsy who did the run! Everybody else did the *walk* with their kids in their wheelchairs. Wow! I was so proud of myself!

The pride I felt was not about boasting or bragging that I accomplished something others did not. It was about how I, as a person and a mother of a child with physical and communication challenges, did not let TJ change our lives because of his circumstances. We include our son in everything we as a family enjoy. TJ came into our lives and has adapted to our lives. We remain being who we are collectively, and individually.

And that especially goes for getting exercise. I force myself to get out of the house. If TJ had his way, he and I would sit in front of the television all day long while he slept in his wheelchair next to me. He is fairly content and happy on those days. When I'm up moving around, though, he's not sure where I am or what I'm going to do next—making him nervous. If I'm not sitting next to him, then he's thinking, *She's getting dressed, she's getting ready, there's going to be someone else here, she's going to leave me, I'm not going with her.* He doesn't trust what's going on. As long as I'm sitting there with him, he's confident that he's not going to be left behind or with a babysitter.

He wasn't always like that. When he was younger he had the normalcy of going to school. He's just like everyone else in that respect. You get used to doing the same thing day-in and day-out, and TJ was used to the everyday routine.

If I don't keep myself in shape, how will I have the physical ability to get TJ up, dressed, and out the door? It is hard. It is a hassle. Yes, sitting home would be easier. But who really wants to do that all day every day?

After the run, I decided to do the walk as well. It was a pretty flat, straight walk, but there were a couple of little inclines and declines. I had two people on the walk ask, "Would you like me to help you? Do you want me to push him for a while and I'll spot you?" Of course I said no. I would say probably 85 percent of the time people are very generous.

When the walk was over, and because it was such a beautiful day, I decide that TJ and I were going to continue our walk and cross a new bridge in Portland named the Tilikum Crossing, Bridge of the People. It serves light rail, city busses, bicycles, emergency vehicles, and pedestrians—regular cars and trucks are not allowed. When you're standing back and looking at the bridge, you see the angle—just as in yoga when you arch your back and the position is called a bridge, this bridge has an arch to it.

It didn't occur to me that there would be an uphill walk, I was just ready to continue walking and enjoying the day. Suddenly I realized that I had to push TJ uphill. He weighs probably 120 pounds and his chair another 100 pounds. I was head down, arms extended, and pushing this heavy contraption up the hill. To have people ask if

I wanted help, well, it just touches your heart. That very gesture lets you know there is amazing humanity in our world. I really do believe TJ brings out the kindness and the charity in all who meet him. Most of the time I take it for what it is. There have only been a few times when I was in a bad mood and did not accept as kindly and graciously as I could have.

I get tired of the fact that to run to the store to get a gallon of milk and a loaf of bread is a twenty-five-minute ordeal, not a five-minute quick trip. I have to get TJ into the van, find an appropriate parking spot, get TJ out of the van, hold the entry door open and push him inside with one hand… Imagine my mood if it's raining!

As handsome as TJ is, he's still scary to little children. They're not frightened to the point that they run away, but he absolutely stops them dead in their tracks, and they stare intently. Older children sometimes run into a wall or a pole backwards because they can't stop watching us long enough to turn around to see where they're going. I know it's because his arms are out to the side and they're in that "W" shape. His fingers are bent and they're pointed out and extended. Because he startles and frightens some kids, it makes them uncomfortable to be around him and not sure how to behave.

These are the times when I just want to go "Bleeahh!" like a monster. I'll say to TJ, "I swear, I'm going to get a button, a ventriloquist-type button that I'll push to make it look like you're doing a monster-type scream." But those times are very few and far between. I don't wish anyone any harm, and I don't want to truly scare anyone, but some days I've just had it with the stares, wanting to scream myself. The irritability never lasts long.

As I watched the other kids who were at the Walk, Roll, or Run, I had to do a thank you to God for giving me this handsome young man who is severely disabled, even though he isn't able to maneuver his own electric wheelchair, having to be pushed. His head wasn't down, his face wasn't contorted—He is a beautiful young man in my opinion.

These are the times when I am taken back to when TJ was born and the doctor wanted to tell both me and Tony that our baby had a high risk of having cerebral palsy. The vision I had back then, as mentioned above, was contorted faces and misshapen heads, and I was just devastated. I thought, *Of all the disabilities in the world, this is the cruelest. These kids may be just fine mentally, but their bodies are so disfigured.* I also remember thinking, *Oh my gosh, You can't do this to me.*

TJ is not your typical-looking cerebral palsy model due to his good-looking face, yet he won't be in a national ad campaign for any kind of recognition or awareness. Organizations still look for, and promote, the darling, blond-haired, blue-eyed little girl for fundraising efforts. Unfortunately the real world does not look that pretty to these kids.

One of the more frustrating parts of living in a handicapped world is finding a place to park. I know that many of you may scratch your head thinking, *But I've seen plenty of designated parking spots at various shopping establishments. It's the normal Joe who can't find a vacant spot.* But the meaning of *handicap* is being watered down to the faintest suggestion of disadvantage. Doctors are authorizing requests to the DMV for special parking placards almost as quickly as they are handing out antibiotics! Because these privileges are over-issued, I often have to drive around for quite a while trying to find the spot labeled "Van Accessible." This extra-wide striped zone allows me to drop the ramp to unload my son's wheelchair. It's not just a great spot at the front that counts.

I have an idea for changing the handicapped parking rules so there are different spaces for different levels of affliction. For instance, I don't have to be five feet from the front door, and neither does TJ, because he's in a wheelchair. We just need some extra space. We can be five rows back, in the purple zone, so the people on crutches or who have arthritis can park in the yellow zone close to the front door of the store. Maybe somebody with different needs gets a green parking space which is close but not right up front.

Makes sense, does it not? We've all seen the seemingly able-bodied dude in the modified truck with twenty-five-foot-diameter tires that sits ten feet off the ground get the closest spot to the entrance of a store, have we not?

Sometimes I have to take up two parking spots, and I'm always afraid someone will get mad and key my van, not caring about the reason I had to take two spots. Even when I find a place way, way in the back of the parking lot, I often return to find that somebody has parked right next to me. Why wouldn't they? I'm in a regular parking spot, after all. Then I have to park TJ in his wheelchair somewhere that is safe, pull my van out, quickly put the ramp down, and hurriedly get TJ in the van before other cars come along.

That is just how a day of shopping can go for me. I will do one or two errands out of an entire string of errands I want to run, and I am completely exhausted. "I'll do the rest tomorrow after Tony gets home."

One day Tony and I were at a restaurant, with TJ in his wheelchair, and our grandson. Through the window I watched an older woman with a young girl—they could have been mother and daughter or caregiver and care recipient; I didn't know them, yet can't imagine why anybody would do this for anybody else but their own child. She got this child into the front seat of her car and then placed pillows and various items that could act as cushions around the young girl. Then she put on a pair of gloves to dismantle the wheelchair. She put the apparatus in the backseat of the car, placing her purchases in and around the wheelchair.

It was a whole process. As I sat and watched it all unfold, I wanted to walk out there to where she was parked and give her the keys to our van and say, "Look, you push this button, a ramp comes out, you wheel your child in there, you get in the van, and you're gone."

I did what she had done for thirteen years. We could finally afford a wheelchair-accessible van when TJ turned thirteen years old. The day we got that van was the greatest day of my life.

I want to give other parents that kind of joy. Tony and I have decided to begin a foundation through which we can give wheelchair-accessible vans to those deserving caregivers and parents who wrangle with kids and wheels far too much.

Walkers take the easiest route through life's ups and downs. Runners see the problems and push through as fast as possible. Wheelers, however, have accomplished a great deal by having come out of their problems with solutions for not only themselves, but to pass on to walkers and runners.

CHAPTER 14
Find Joy

Whatever is going on in your life, you don't need to lose who you are underneath. Retain your identity—the person you truly are. Sometimes it's easy to get wrapped up in victim mode, forgetting how strong you are or not caring about what someone else might be going through and thinking, *Heck with the world, it's my turn to moan!* It might be!

Becky Ballard shared her story with me after we became neighbors. I knew her parents when I was her age and was so surprised to see these friends from my past carrying belongings into the home beside mine. Becky is a beautiful young mother with four children. She lived in my neighborhood for years before I was told the extent of her trials. Just last year she said good-by to her oldest son as he left to serve his mission. She is hoping and praying she will be alive in two years when he returns.

People now share their personal issues via social media. Do they think that gives them notoriety? I think people in the past felt more pride in handling their problems themselves and dealing with them behind closed doors. The backside of that is that people didn't get the help they needed because they were ashamed to talk about their trials. It's a two-sided coin, for sure.

I decided to ask Becky her thoughts about sharing the journey of her latest battle with cancer on Facebook. The reasoning behind the shares, the photos, and the posts was not "Oh, please cry for me," it was so people would *pray* for her and so they could stay informed and up to date on her welfare. She did not want to elicit fear, but hope. She believes that people need to know that you will survive and come out stronger on the other side of the trial—and that you are not alone.

One other piece of wisdom Becky shared was that if you worry too much and dread your trials, you'll miss your joy. The joy she feels when she celebrates her "all clear" tests is a testimony of her faith and her belief that she is being watched over by our Heavenly Father. Putting your trials into perspective is good practice. You may not want to dwell on the bad, certainly, but your happy times, your joys, are going to pass by just as quickly as everything else. By placing the focus on your joys, the trials that continue just might be a little less painful to endure.

The plan of salvation, however, requires those moments of despair. If you don't have sorrow, you will never know or experience joy. But it's not a game, and there is no winner. You don't gain joy or win the trial gold medal just because your trial is harder than my trial. Yet there are people who put their trials on an invisible graph to rate who has the worst affliction. *But wait! You're not a Syrian refugee who is carrying your baby to a new life!* You can see that kind of thing on social media all the time. Someone will post a picture of starving babies with a caption reading, "Now, tell me about your bad day."

You must have perspective, however, about your pain and unhappiness. You do get to be sad. You do get to be down. You do get to be discouraged. You have that right. But there's no reason to make life's typical annoyances into cataclysmic events. As hard as your experience must have been for you, ask yourself, "Is this trial one to be shared publicly?" Ask yourself these three questions before you push "Post": 1) What really caused my pain? 2) Will my post appear to be angry and judging? 3) Am I publicly humiliating someone in my family?

It's natural to compare our trials with those of others, but there are some that are just too personal to be shared, just as there are blessings that perhaps shouldn't be shared. Your personal trial, the spiritual experience you had, or the message you received from seeing or feeling someone from beyond the veil was possibly meant for you alone, and no one else is to hear or know about it. Or you might have a strong feeling that others could benefit from hearing about your experience. Only by listening to the Spirit will this be known.

I don't want to negate that we all have bad days. And you don't have to be starving in Rwanda or be diagnosed as terminally ill to be allowed to have a bad day. Trials can be devastating and should be acknowledged as such. Feel free at any time to say, "Life Sucks and This Isn't Fair!" I know that everybody has their baseline. What's hard for one person might not be hard for another. What has to be checked is our offense barometer. When others do not consider our "trial" as catastrophic as we do, it is human nature to retreat or attack.

There are many scriptures that tell us how not to be offended— or not to be offended so easily. David A. Bednar reminds us:

> When we believe or say we have been offended, we usually mean we feel insulted, mistreated, snubbed, or disrespected. And certainly clumsy, embarrassing, unprincipled, and mean-spirited things do occur in our interactions with other people that would allow us to take offense. However, it ultimately is impossible for another person to offend you or to offend me. Indeed, believing that another person offended us is fundamentally false. To be offended is a choice we make; it is not a condition inflicted or imposed upon us by someone or something else. (https://www.lds.org/general-conference/2006/10/and-nothing-shall-offend-them?lang=eng)

I love this teaching. The idea that it is our choice to be offended or hurt works. It works politically. It works religiously. It works with our personal trials. For instance, we shouldn't get offended when someone grunts and turns up their nose because our autistic child is having a meltdown. We must be as patient with the stranger as we ask them to be with us. I believe there is a shiny rule about that somewhere! Golden, if I remember correctly.

It seems we are easily offended these days. I like to remember President Gordon B. Hinkley's statement about the media:

> The amount of venom that spewed from the mouths and pens of the commentators was unbelievable. They were aflame with indignation...The columnists were masters of the written word. With studied art they poured out the sour vinegar of invective and anger, judging as if all wisdom belonged to them. At the conclusion of that week, I too made a negative observation. Said I, "Surely this is the age and place of the gifted pickle sucker." (https://speeches.byu.edu/talks/gordon-b-hinckley_let-heart-troubled/)

President Hinkley was talking about people with sour faces and attitudes. Our media and neighborhoods are full of these people. Perhaps even a few of them sit around our dining room tables. So what do we do? We need to be moderate and concentrate on living the commandments. President Hinkley continued:

> What I am suggesting and asking is that we turn from the negativism that so permeates our society and look for the remarkable good in the land and times in which we live, that we speak of one another's virtues more than we speak of one another's faults, that optimism replace pessimism, that our faith exceed our fears.

Everyone has down days and crying times. But you have two choices—find joy or die in your tears.

Notice that "find peace" is not a choice. If you find peace with your trial, that's all well and good, but you can still be wallowing in your pain. When you choose joy, the misery doesn't disappear altogether—yet you can still be happy. Finding peace means you've settled with the outcome; you've no more work to do in overcoming or getting past the hurt and pain. When you choose joy in the overcoming, you have gained strength.

Why is it that when people have a trial of some kind, the first thing they think of is, "I am experiencing misery, therefore I cannot attend three hours of church. I can't serve others because, HELLO, look what I am having to endure! My prayers have not been answered, my faith is dead. I have to leave my tribe. I have to leave my community. Then I can wallow alone as it is meant to be."

Maybe you've had similar thoughts and questioned your faith during your trials. You may have questions and feel the rustlings of dissent. You question your truths. Your faith in your leaders is shaken.

A person can justify anything they want to. I can only repeat the words of M. Russel Ballard: "We need to experience a continuing conversion by increasing our faith in Jesus Christ and our faithfulness to His Gospel throughout our lives—not just once but regularly."

Alma asked, "And now behold, I say unto you, my brethren [and sisters], if ye have experienced a change of heart, and if ye have felt to sing the song of redeeming love, I would ask, can ye feel so now?…It seems that these things which are not easily measured are of great importance. Stay focused on these simple things, and avoid becoming distracted."

Have you become distracted? We are reminded that the Gospel is simple; but we love things to be hard, don't we? Remember my reference to Pinterest? We like things complicated and hard so we can feel good about our accomplishments. We make excuses to fit the lifestyle we want to live.

Humans on the Earth today love the word *moderately*. We have let that word slip into our lexicon and we throw it around with ease to justify our behavior. But we have been given many instructions from the Lord that do not allow for moderation. We are not told to read our scriptures or pray *moderately*. We are not allowed to drink alcohol or coffee *moderately* if we want to have access to all the ordinances of the priesthood; we are challenged to avoid these substances.

We are allowed to fail but encouraged to try harder. I love the advice from the great prophet Yoda: "Do or do not, there is no TRY!"

People find a god that works with their lifestyle, whatever that might be. They might change religions. They might give up on Jesus Christ and go to Buddha or Mohammad or to idols that work with what they want to do and how they want to live. We often adjust our own Prophets' teachings in accordance with our desires. L. Tom Perry reminds us:

> One of the challenges of this mortal experience is to not allow the stresses and strains of life to get the better of us—to endure the varied seasons of life while remaining positive, even optimistic. Perhaps when difficulties and challenges strike, we should have these hopeful words of Robert Browning etched in our minds: "The best is yet to be."
> ("Rabbi Ben Ezra," in Charles W. Eliot, ed., *The Harvard Classics*, 50 vols., 1909–10, 42:1103)

I often wonder to myself why all the evil is happening in the world. Here in America, our trials seem trivial compared to what is happening elsewhere. My trial is about time and freedom—the physical freedom to do what I want to when I want to. Really? Can I really watch the families stomp through the mud and cold to flee a war-torn country and complain? The world has never been free of turmoil and pandemonium, or from dictators greedy for money, property, or power.

My testimony of prayer has finally reached a more mature level as I have aged and finally recognized how my prayers have been answered. I was finally at a time in my life when I could volunteer for the Portland Oregon Temple. Ordinances and Covenants took on a completely new meaning when I was able to attend weekly and for many hours. One element that I took for granted and previously practiced almost by rote is the prayer roll. People can write down on a list the names of loved ones they want to have included in a group prayer. Strength in numbers, a common plea. Lots of prayers are going out to these people, no matter and whatever their needs.

Because my attendance had increased, so, too, did my requests for prayers to be said for those I love. My aging father's name one week, my children always, the mothers of my grandchildren as their due dates came closer. Of course I always included TJ. What was God's plan for him? I don't know but I always prayed for comfort for him.

During my time of service in the temple I was witness to a miracle in our family. One of my sons who had married the love of his life called Tony and me with the most startling news. Without telling us, he and his wife, who was not a member, had been taking the discussions. With the birth of their baby, my son's heart had been touched. The promise of Elder Orson F. Whitney of the Quorum of the Twelve Apostles in 1929 was manifested in our home. Elder Whitney stated:

> The Prophet Joseph Smith declared—and he never taught more comforting doctrine—that the eternal sealings of faithful parents and the divine promises made to them for valiant service in the Cause of Truth, would save not only themselves, but likewise their posterity. Though some of the sheep may wander, the eye of the Shepherd is upon them, and sooner or later they will feel the tentacles of Divine Providence reaching out after them and drawing

them back to the fold. Either in this life or the life to come, they will return. They will have to pay their debt to justice; they will suffer for their sins; and may tread a thorny path; but if it leads them at last, like the penitent Prodigal, to a loving and forgiving father's heart and home, the painful experience will not have been in vain. Pray for your careless and disobedient children; hold on to them with your faith. Hope on, trust on, till you see the salvation of God. (http://scriptures.byu.edu/gc-historical/1929-A.pdf)

We had prayed for his family and had asked others to pray for them as well by placing his name on the prayer roll. My son told me, "We made the decision that we wanted our children to know God. We wanted to attend church as a family. I confessed that though I had not been practicing my religion, I knew it was right and I could never attend another church." His wife agreed to take the discussions.

They hadn't told anyone of their discussion when one evening missionaries showed up at their door. They asked if they could talk to them about the Gospel. My son received a phone call from his wife: "The missionaries are here. They want to know if they can come in." My son recognized this answer to prayers and they began their study.

That Christmas my son's wife was baptized. One year later, just weeks after the birth of their second child, the family was sealed together for time and all eternity. This was an answer to prayers, no doubts, but it was also my son and his wife's desire to teach their children in the way they were taught. My daughter-in-law is a special gift who is in tune with the Lord. She turned to God when her life was in turmoil even before she met my son. She recognized the Holy Spirit when it testified to her because she had experience with prayer and knew.

Prayer is like exercise. When our muscles have been trained, they create memory. Even when we slack off, it doesn't take long for our muscles to remember what we want them to do. If we take a break from working out, we often have to begin from the beginning, and it takes a while before we gain back what we lost. This is also true of prayer. My son and his wife took some time off, but they returned and now their children bow their heads, fold their arms, and repeat their innocent pleadings to Heavenly Father.

Not all of my children have embraced the Gospel in their adult lives, but I know what I have been promised, and my faith has been strengthened by what I have been given so far. Life is eternal, and so will be our progress and our perfection. President Brigham Young taught:

> The first great principle that ought to occupy the attention of mankind, that should be understood by the child and the adult, and which is the main spring of all action, whether people understand it or not, is the principle of improvement. The principle of increase, of exaltation, of adding to that we already possess, is the grand moving principle and cause of the actions of the children of men. No matter what their pursuits are, in what nation they were born, with what people they have been associated, what religion they profess, or what politics they hold, this is the main spring of the actions of the people, embracing all the powers necessary in performing the duties of life.
> (http://scriptures.byu.edu/jod/jodhtml.php?vol=02&disc=20)

Is your life improving, even in a small way? Find the small things that are improving, even if it is that your houseplants are thriving or you got through dinner without anyone throwing food. There is increase in your life. When you find it and celebrate, it helps you get through those bad days as a victor rather than a victim.

CHAPTER 15

Boots on the Ground

I will never be the next Wayne Dyer or any new-age guru of deep thoughts. Stuart Smalley is not my icon. I don't look into the mirror daily and repeat words of affirmation. I'm one more on the side of thinking affirmation is a scary Kool Aid that we've all been counseled to drink daily.

Why do I believe this? Because I don't trust my opinion of me. I would rather receive affirmation from someone who can look past my wrinkles and cellulite. I would rather receive affirmation from someone who sees in me the perfection that I will never be able to actually obtain.

Who is that person here on earth? My helpmate is pretty good but I rarely trust his observations of most things. A good example is my latest comment: "Honey, that car is not tan! Duh, it's obviously celery!" I can only trust one opinion of my worth, that of my Father in Heaven. (My earthly father thinks I'm quite the bee's knees, but he's old.)

In a conference talk, Elder O. Vincent Haleck reminded us:

The Savior saw more in those humble fishermen whom He called to follow Him than they initially saw in themselves; He saw a vision of who they could become. (https://www.lds.org/general-conference/2012/04/having-the-vision-to-do?lang=eng)

How do we become all that we can become? By seeking guidance and then taking action!

I never have been able to grasp the idea of meditation. Quietly cleansing my thoughts is never going to happen for me. I like thinking about stuff. I love prayer because *pray* is a verb. It requires action. The best part about prayer is you are allowed to talk! My favorite activity. You can whisper-talk, think-in-your-brain talk, or yell if you want to!

Then, after we talk to God, we are instructed to be quiet and listen. That is the hard part, but at least we have direction, right? We know what we are listening for.

We have been taught to pray constantly. In Psalms 55:27 we read, "Evening, and morning, and at noon, will I pray, and cry aloud; and He shall hear my voice."

When we have prayed; thanked our Heavenly Father for EVERYTHING; perhaps slipped in a request as in a prayer for healing, a prayer for relief from sorrow or trials, a prayer for direction, or whatever your heart needs and what has brought you to your knees; then we are told to listen. Listen for the still, small voice. Listen for confirmation, listen for an idea, listen for and wait for a feeling of comfort.

Then, and here is the great part… we are told to get off our knees and go to work! Move it! I like to move it, move it! *Madagascar,* one of my favorite movies!

There is a phrase being thrown around lately: "Boots on the ground." I'm here to deploy all of you and to reaffirm that you've got to have boots on the ground. *Faith* is an action word! In all the scriptures we read of people in action: Moses, Abinidi, Alma, Noah… I'm stopping because I would have to list them all. Every success story in or out of the scriptures is a tale of perseverance and action. Let's just all say it. Turn to the person on your right and say to them, "My life stinks right now, and you?" No one is going to take hardship off your plate. What is your plan? What's the next maneuver? You've got to be your own army.

My husband and I had the amazing experience of standing on the beaches of Normandy. I have never been a history buff or generally interested in the topic of war, but I was fascinated to learn of this event. I watched every WWII movie or documentary I could get my hands on for months after returning from our trip.

Do you know why I was so fascinated? Because nothing worked out the way it was supposed to. Brilliant minds, experienced soldiers, experts in the field of battle and war got it wrong! *Over and over again!* But men went into battle without any assurance that they would not be killed. Amazing miracles occurred and lives were lost and saved simultaneously. There were both tragedies and joy.

A lot of books are written by people whose trials are over, like the ones about surviving a horrible accident or natural disaster. The authors are so relieved to be done with that horrible event that they can now reflect and see the great lessons they learned. There is nothing wrong with these books. However, for some of us, our trial doesn't end. It endures.

What about you? Perhaps your trial is still ongoing. Perhaps your life seems to mirror Job's. While today I celebrated the healing of one friend diagnosed with cancer, I attended the funeral of a young mother of five who lost her battle.

Do you have an autistic child? The rate today is one out of every sixty-eight children born will be diagnosed with autism spectrum disorder. Autism comes in many colors. Some children are able to advance and live independent lives. Some require assistance their entire lives. That trial, like many other disabilities, never goes away. Many never find a cure for their hardship. There is no chemotherapy or surgery for many physical disabilities.

I learned greatly from a devotional I came across that was given at Brigham Young University by Elaine S. Marshall. Her words rang so true in my heart, but more important, they untangled threads of confusion in my mind. She teaches us: "Healing hurts. Life hurts.

Healing really only begins when we face the hurt in its full force and then grow through it with all the strength of our soul."

For a short time I was able to serve in the Portland Oregon Temple as a temple worker. Although my service lasted only a few short years due to family obligations, my ability to spend hours in the temple every week as a worker and not a patron left grooves in my life like a record.

Sitting quietly while attending our weekly three-hour block of service on Sundays demands at least a gold star on my chart of achievements in the sky. Ordinance work performed in the temples requires even more grown-up-type quiet sitting. Then on top of that it's repetitive—one of the reasons I don't craft. I don't like doing the same thing over and over again. Attending the temple requires a great deal of mature behavior. This is hard!

But I soon discovered that if you are a temple *worker*, you get to move! You get to talk! You even get to eat in the cafeteria! Woo hoo! It was like my favorite subject in high school all over again. You start out your shift with a pep assembly, everyone changes into their team uniforms, girls are hanging with girls and boys are hanging with boys, and then you have to go to class and do your work. But you get lunch and recess with your friends! It's the best! I could spend six hours once a week there easily—the best school in the world! I hated to leave its hallowed hallways, and my, oh my, my six hours of measly nothing reaped tons of blessings on our family.

I loved everything about working in the temple. I had found an angel to care for TJ to make it easy for me to do my temple work. This tiny Hispanic friend from Mexico came into our family and into our hearts. I have never seen service or compassion demonstrated so vividly as I did in this woman. Her whole life was spent serving others. She married young, worshipped and adored her three children, cared for her brothers and sisters, served the needy at her church, and sat by the bedside of a dying friend after she finished her shift caring for TJ. She loved to make others happy and she couldn't bear the thought of disappointing anyone.

That, however, created a problem when something in her life would take her away from helping me. She didn't want to tell me— she was sick with sorrow that she would be letting me down—so she always waited until the very last minute to give me the bad news.

"I have bad news," she would begin, her eyes beginning to moisten. "Oh no, what is wrong?" I would ask. "I have to have surgery on my leg and will not be able to care for your son for a while," she would tell me. "No problem, of course," I would say. "When is your surgery?" Then she would say, inevitably, "Tomorrow."

TOMORROW!!!! I would be screaming in my head. We would hug and I would say good luck and then after the door closed I would fall on the sofa and sob! I would call Tony, not to turn to him for comfort or solace but truly just to let him know how angry I was not only at her for waiting so long to tell me so that I had to make other arrangements at the last minute, but to subliminally let him know that I was mad at him for being able to have a life that didn't revolve around child care! I was secretly going to make him suffer, too.

Then he always called my bluff and won the hand. "Don't worry, Honey. I'll watch TJ on Tuesday nights so you can continue your temple work." Dang, foiled again! Kindness always trumps anger. It took a while to make this work, but we were able to do it for another year or so, at least until Tony was called to be the bishop and then there was no way to make it work. He couldn't give me Tuesday nights any longer. I had to quit my temple service.

When things like that happen in our forty-something years of togetherness, my selfish resentment comes back—the resentment that my role as mother doesn't have a time line. I resent the fact that Tony rarely has to tell somebody, "I'm sorry, I can't do that anymore. I have to care for my disabled son." He has never had to decline church callings, work, or golf, or turn anybody down because he has a child he has to take care of.

I start feeling sorry for myself. I hate everybody. I hate the whole world. I feel, once again, that my life has no purpose; that something that was mine has been taken away. I get depressed. And at times I think, "That's it, God? You just want me to stay home and sit on the couch and watch *Turner Classic Movies* all day long? Change TJ's bed and feed him and take care of him, and that's it? That's what my whole life is to be? To support my husband in all of his adventures—the many adventures of Tony—while it's my job to stay home and take care of Tony Junior? Stand by my man? That's my worth? Where is that patriarchal blessing? I know there was more in there, after the line that reads, "mother…bla bla…children…"

Having the opportunity to talk to others every week on my radio show who have gone through trials, absorbing how they survived and learning from them, has been a great outlet, providing many lessons.

My show usually airs on Monday, and I can ride that high for at least three days. I'm somewhere center by Thursday, and usually by Friday I'm that Mylar balloon in the corner slowly loosing air, trying to stay afloat. Sundays fill me back up and by Monday I'm back in the air!

I love learning every day, trying to find affirmation outside myself and my life's story. I'm hoping to have at least thirty more years to try to perfect this. If I can't find perfection, then my next wish is for that funny form of forgetfulness that seems to sweep over us when we age. We start saying things like "Oh, those two lovebirds; never heard a cross word out of them in sixty-five years of marriage." My response to that? You weren't home.

If I can help you not wallow in self-pity, then we'll both be happy campers. And that's what my purpose seems to be these days. Not only do I have to make lemonade out of my lemons, but I have to figure out how to remove the pulp that is mucking up my straw! Many days I'm so glad I made a covenant to not drink alcohol, because I can tell by my M&M stash that I would be a closet drinker.

Though I have a strong testimony of the power of prayer, I can't say I have had many "TADA" moments. Just a few. I usually feel like God is answering my prayers by saying, "Hey you, get off of my cloud, go serve someone and forget about yourself."

Obviously if he were to pass on, our entire life would change as well. Maybe we could serve a mission as a couple. Maybe we could take the grandkids hiking through the Grand Canyon. Maybe my husband and I could finally be us again and not Mom and Dad.

But I wonder truly what is going through TJ's mind that he can't share? Does he yell in his mind, *My hips ache all day sitting in one position. Please check my legs; that medical tape you put on has latex in it and my legs are breaking out in a horrible itchy rash!* His pain must be horrible on some days. I hate to watch my children suffer. Even when it is self-inflicted, my heart breaks and I want to offer relief. When he goes to be with Heavenly Father, he will be relieved of a lifetime of suffering. That will be a day to rejoice, as well as to mourn.

This prayer has not been necessarily answered, yet maybe it was answered—and the answer is that I'm sharing TJ with the world because people are so drawn to him. He's a peacemaker, bringing smiles to everyone in the mall, a movie theater, or wherever he happens to be.

I almost hate to say this because it has become a cliché, but many say they need to share their story to help others with their own stories, and I do believe that TJ has a story that needs to be told. This just may be his trial, and telling his story could very well help other families in their struggle and trial of caring for a child with cerebral palsy or another affliction.

The stories that affect me are truths, like those of people who don't want to be called heroes just because they showed up for chemotherapy and ultimately beat cancer. What about the child who showed up for her surgery and chemotherapy, yet she died? What is she? A loser? She didn't fight hard enough? Just because God called her home doesn't make her weak or a loser. I would wager everybody going through cancer is a fighter. Everybody. And those who died fought just as hard as those who lived to tell their story.

That's where you have to come back to your own thankfulness and grace, recognizing that the illness, or whatever circumstance it was, was definitely a blessing. Yet were you *not* blessed because your child died? At times I hate to use the word *blessed* for just this reason.

Usually I don't ask for a lot in my prayers. They are mostly prayers of thankfulness. I'm almost afraid to ask for anything because if the answer doesn't go my way, I think there must be a reason. And it's not that God is punishing me or you—so let's keep going.

You are entitled to a pity-party. But friends' might last a week while yours is only a day and a half. The size and length of the pity-party depends on the event causing the party.

Many trials we have are out of our control due to another's free agency. My mind and heart are often returned to the story of Timothy Ballard. His story is told in an article by Jamie Armstrong called "Rescuing Children from Sex Slavery: One Mormon's Inspired Mission." Jaime begins his article with this scene: "On a balmy February afternoon in the poverty-stricken country of Haiti, Timothy Ballard is thrown to the ground and handcuffed by local law enforcement. Lifting his head from the asphalt, he watches as the woman who just sold him two young children—a brother and sister ages 2 and 3—for $15,000 apiece is hauled away by police."

The article goes on to tell Timothy's story; how he rescues these children and how he relies on constant prayer to guide him. Please look up this article. These are not these children's trials; this horrible practice of selling and using children for sexual pleasure is not anything sanctioned or put on this earth to teach us anything accept to recognize how not following the Lord's commandments can destroy souls. Timothy is quoted: "The problem of child sex slavery is 100 percent the societal consequence of our pornographic world…Pornography is a drug. Adult pornography is marijuana, and child pornography is the cocaine. When people move on to child pornography, eventually they want the real thing." It's a choice.

In the past my faith never wandered, but my understanding of how prayer works was confused. People would stand up in church and give these simplistic accounts such as "I lost my contact lens [or the diamond out of my ring]. I prayed it would be found. And when I took out the garbage, I noticed a sparkle on the ground. I just knew God had answered my prayer and led me to the lost lens [or diamond]." I remember thinking, *Really? A child has gone missing. I'm sure the child's parents have prayed, begged, demanded that God find their daughter like Elizabeth Smart was found. God can find lost baseball hats but not little girls?*

But then it happened to me. A simple, silly thing happened. Something I needed to find and was beginning to panic over was found—oddly found somewhere I didn't expect it to be—and I understood. It was a gift; my lost item did not go missing because of someone else's free agency. It wasn't stolen. No one had to bear the consequences of my lapse in memory. It was a gentle reminder that God knows what I need; a gentle tap that said, "I'm still here. Oh, and by the way, here is that item you misplaced."

I cannot begin to understand the pain that many people are enduring today. I only have what I have, but have I done any good in the world today? Maybe instead of self-affirmation—telling ourselves how great we are—we should look into the mirror and ask ourselves, "Is my sorrow really a trial or merely a slight pang in my side?" Not everyone has a victim song that needs to be sung. Elder Jeffrey R. Holland reminds us:

In striving for some peace and understanding in these difficult matters, it is crucial to remember that we are living—and chose to live—in a fallen world where for divine purposes our pursuit of godliness will be tested and tried again and again. Of greatest assurance in God's plan is that a Savior was promised, a Redeemer, who through our faith in Him would lift us triumphantly over those tests and trials, even though the cost to do so would be unfathomable for both the Father who sent Him and the Son who came. It is only an appreciation of this divine love that will make our own lesser suffering first bearable, then understandable, and finally redemptive. So how do you best respond when mental or emotional challenges confront you or those you love? Above all, never lose faith in your Father in Heaven, who loves you more than you can comprehend. (https://www.lds.org/general-conference/2013/10/like-a-broken-vessel?lang=eng)

As President Monson said to the Relief Society sisters so movingly last Saturday evening:

That love never changes…It is there for you when you are sad or happy, discouraged or hopeful. God's love is there for you whether or not you feel you deserve [it]. It is simply always there. Never, ever doubt that, and never harden your heart. Faithfully pursue the time-tested devotional practices that bring the Spirit of the Lord into your life. Seek the counsel of those who hold keys for your spiritual well-being. (https://www.lds.org/general-conference/2013/10/we-never-walk-alone?lang=eng)

Boots on the ground, ladies—faith that the army of angels we are promised is truly watching over us. They can't move our arms and legs for us; we aren't puppets. We have to have faith just as those young boys who wandered into the cold ocean and onto the beaches of Normandy had.

Lieutenant Colonel Robert L. Woverton, commanding officer of 3rd battalion at Normandy, said, "We do not know or seek what our fate will be. We ask only this, that if die we must, that we die as men would die, without complaining, without pleading and safe in the feeling that we have done our best for what we believed was right."

We moms have our boots on the ground every day. We are in action, doing our best for our families. Some days those actions are laudable; others days, maybe not so much. However, our Heavenly Father has given us the tools of prayer, endurance, and faith to use as we travel this fallen world. We see suffering close up when our child cries or our elderly parent ends up in the hospital. They need us to be strong, even when we feel weak.

You can do it. "Boots" come in various styles. I highly recommend those made by Steve Madden and *greatly* discourage Crocs, but choose for yourself, and start walking. By the way, you never walk alone!

CHAPTER 16

My Recipe for Lemonade

The preverbal old saying, "When life hands you lemons, make lemonade," is maybe annoying to hear at times, and yet such simple good advice. It's so simple, in fact, that that might be what makes it annoying.

I hardly hear anyone order a simple lemonade anymore. Strawberry, mint, mango—you name it. Lots of things are getting mixed in to make good old-fashioned lemonade quite the fancy drink. They have even added alcohol, and it's now called "hard lemonade." Does anyone ever say "If your life is hard, make hard lemonade"? No.

What is your favorite life-to-lemonade recipe? Let me share mine.

Ingredient one: You must do everything in your power to stay healthy. If you are sick, you are in prison. Who will care for you, your children, your career, your joy? In this day—this new twenty-first century—I doubt that any of us, male or female, will not be touched by a disability.

My oldest daughter has four children, one of whom has been diagnosed with autism. Maybe you have two little girls who play with Barbie dolls all day long and color within the lines. This makes you believe you are the parent extraordinaire! You may wonder why other parents are complaining. I say to you now, just wait. If it hasn't yet happened, your time is coming. Most children defy their parents' ideals at some point. It's just life. It even happened to God, so why should you be exempt?

I didn't have an autistic child, but I have grandchildren who are autistic. I didn't lose my husband in a car accident, but my daughter has. You must be prepared for anything that might come, that other shoe to drop. You may think you have your life figured out, but reality tells a different story. If you haven't had a disappointing chapter yet, keep reading.

I do not have the luxury of taking my health for granted. I've tried it; no one stepped in to relieve me of my duties! I tried to prolong an illness for as long as I could, but I guess my acting ability is lacking. I wasn't totally ignored, but I soon realized that lying in bed was not going to be my lot. Maybe temporarily, but only for a few short days. Foiled again! I have to be healthy for TJ, and that's stressful and scary, but I do the best I can.

Running used to be something I enjoyed. But for some reason I can't make myself do it anymore. I begin with the same routine, a little stretching, a warm-up walk… okay, go… I walk a little faster… GO… I CAN'T MAKE MYSELF BEGIN THE RUN! All I can do is walk. And that frightens me. Am I getting old? My mind says run, my body is still walking! What's up? How will I be able to care for TJ? How will I be able to pick him up? I will have to hire someone to come in and bathe and dress him in the morning—probably in the next few years. But that's my reality: I will have to have help someday!

Oh, the pain!

So I make myself take TJ for a walk or get us in the van and go do something, just to get out of the house. You cannot just sit home with your handicapped child. That's not a life. You can't. And you don't have to. There are a lot of people and programs that want to give back, that want to help you get out of the house, to have a life.

You might be like me in that the hardest thing is to accept help. Even when people ask me if they can help me with TJ, I am often too proud, and say, "No, I got it." This is wrong. I am denying them the opportunity to do something good, and denying myself the opportunity to receive. Do you ever say no to help from others? It is good to sometimes let people help in whatever way they want to. Let them come over and sit with your kid while you go for a walk. What? You live in a scary neighborhood so you can't just go outside for a walk? Then you have to change that up.

If you continually make excuses as to why you can't go for a walk or take a break from your child long enough to get respite, then what's the alternative? Are you going to stay home and suffer with cabin fever, get depressed, develop diabetes? What are your choices? How can *you* solve your problem? Sounds too easy, I know. But if not you, then who? The question you have to ask yourself when you say you can't do something as simple as going for a walk is: If not that, then what?

Stay healthy.

Ingredient two: Be strong spiritually. When prepared spiritually you have a built-in shock absorber during times of trial. Does your spirituality make you immune to the devastation or the circumstances of life? No, of course not. Just because you are a faithful, obedient, scripture-reading, prayerful person does not mean that something painful won't happen to you. But it is your armor, your defense, your solace. It might be your only refuge.

In many religions, parishioners are used to being spiritually fed. They rely on the pastor to teach and to uplift them. If there is an event, members are asked to volunteer, to sign up to help. In our lay church we don't have paid ministry, and therefore everyone is asked to contribute in some way. You are specifically asked to volunteer in some way, and often not in a position that you would choose for yourself or that you even have skills in!

You're asked to serve with other humans, and invariably your teammates or co-volunteers have odd personality traits or they have forgotten that it's not a paid position and that others are volunteering their time. Albeit they are still your brothers and sisters. They might actually act like your brother or sister whom you often beat up or get into tussles with! But because we are asked to serve in various positions throughout our lifetimes, we soon learn that this is what life is all about: learning to get along, learning from one another, learning to love those we… aaaa… don't!

To survive big and small trials, you must have your own testimony, your own relationship with God. Not your parents' testimony, not your bishop's, not your Young Women president's testimony. Be careful not to get caught up in other people's stories of their relationship with Christ. I have often found it difficult to relate to others' stories. I have my own struggles, and I have to find my own peace. You have to have your own relationship with God that gives you a personal revelation—this is the most important thing about being a Christian: being able to sit back and listen to the voice that is speaking to you directly.

Your calling is not your testimony; it isn't even about you. It's an opportunity to serve. Don't be discouraged, or the opposite—puffed-up, about the job you are asked to perform or volunteer for in the Gospel. It's all just service, folks. Give it your all.

Ingredient three: Be in tune. Be aware of what is going on in your family as much as you can. I was not always aware and in tune. I often reflect back and realize that I thought my family was in a bubble, protected from outside influences, because we thought we had the basics down. I was naive and believed that bad things could not happen to our family because we went to church, we didn't have pornography in the home, we didn't use drugs or alcohol, and our caregivers were from our same religion. I wasn't listening because I thought I had nothing to hear. Through the gift of the Holy Ghost, my mind was opened and I was made aware of my blindness.

Listen to a God who knows all, and don't assume that you have it all figured out. Don't be afraid to question authority or the actions of even those you hold in high esteem. Listen to the subtle messages of children. I didn't hear; my eyes were blinded by youth and what I thought was innocence. Be in tune with your gut, with your own instincts.

If you are truly inspired to peek inside when you find your daughter's diary, do it! When she says she hates her whole family and wishes she could run away, remember what you were like at that age—there's a good possibility she is fourteen years old and that is all. You may remember how you hated your mother, too, at that age. I think every daughter has felt that way at least once in her life.

I know that my Heavenly Father had a plan for me. That plan included having parents who were snoopy! My father went into my room to hang some curtains one Saturday when I was about sixteen. There on my bedside table was my diary. This man despises contention and rule-breaking. He is at the least a compulsive rule-follower. He felt inspired to open the pages and read a few. There, in detail, I had laid out my recent activities with my best friend.

Needless to say, that friendship was ended. I was punished and forbidden to associate with her again. Her parents were contacted, but they didn't believe any of my parents' information. My best friend was taken away from me and I hated them for a brief while, but I know now that I was being watched over. I was at a crossroads and Heavenly Father, through my loving parents, picked me up and pointed me in the right direction. This has happened to me often. Obviously I have a stubborn streak and demand more intervention than most!

If your children's personalities have changed or you feel like something is amiss, act on it. Be willing to lose their love for a while; they will return and thank you one day, and even if they don't (there is that free agency thing again), you have a stewardship.

You might need to be prepared to stand up for them and do what you need to do for them. Find a mental health professional if your child needs to be on a different kind of path. Needing therapy is not devastating. You are doing what is best for them.

It's your job to know your child. Do what you need to do, and then be okay with the choice you made.

Ingredient four: Become the advocate. Learn how to speak up for yourself and your child and not just remain quietly in the corner hoping things will be better. It's a different world today, and we must be willing to fight for our families, and maybe with our families, to do the right thing.

Speaking up for myself has been a learning process for me, too. I've watched talented, loving people advocate for TJ at his school and at the hospital. I've been able to stand aside and say, "Wow, thank you." In years past I never did that and did not know I could do that. So now, as an official sage, I tell my children, "You can ask for anything you want. You might not get it, but you can ask." Learn from what I did wrong and what I didn't do. When I finally let people tell me things and accepted that I was no longer acquiescing, I became my own advocate and learned to find things out for myself.

I don't trust that others have my passion for my family and their needs. Why should they? I don't even trust the store clerk with something as simple as whether they have the ribbon I want in stock. I drive to the store to find out. Why I don't call first? Do you think some teenaged chick honestly cares enough to walk away from the phone to actually look on the shelf to see if the ribbon you want is there? You'll get either of two answers:

1) "No, we don't have your ribbon." They didn't actually check to see, so the call was useless. That also goes for asking when you get to the store. I only ask after a bit of scavenging on my own.

2) "Yes, we have your ribbon." But do they? Do they have the red ribbon you described or just red ribbon?

I guess I have trust issues! Either way, I won't believe them. So I'll drive there to look myself. Maybe it's because I enjoy the hunt or maybe employees truly are lazy. Regardless, I will not be assured until I've done the work myself.

It's no different with your kids. You call a doctor's office or an agency requesting help and ask for information about a program you heard about, only to be told it doesn't exist. Don't stop. Find out more. Ask to speak to a supervisor. Call back another day and speak to someone else.

Here is the most important rule, however: Don't be a jerk. Be polite. Work within the system. They might not be spitting in your food but they might accidently lose your file if you're too much of a pain. As my grandmother always said, "You catch more flies with honey than you do with vinegar." Not sure that is true. Actually you probably catch more flies with garbage, but let's not go there!

Ingredient five: Find strength in the solution, not the struggle. There is a psychological condition called *learned helplessness*. Kendra Cherry, a psychology expert, describes it like this: "Learned helplessness occurs when an animal is repeatedly subjected to an aversive stimulus that it cannot escape. Eventually, the animal will stop trying to avoid the stimulus and behave as if it is utterly helpless to change the situation. Even when opportunities to escape are presented, this learned helplessness will prevent any action."

Are you suffering from learned helplessness? If you feel you have no control over a situation, it can be easy to slip into thinking that things will never get better, and you stop trying. This is not something a strong mother can afford to do.

With the release of his new book, *A Full Life*, Jimmy Carter is currently making the circuit of radio and television show interviews. After hearing one of the interviews on NPR, what struck me was the relationship Mr. Carter has with his wife, Rosalynn. He spoke of how he and Rosalynn decided to write a book together. The agreement was that she was going to write a chapter and he was going to write a chapter. He said that it almost destroyed them. I'll paraphrase it this way:

> I would write a chapter and give it to her to edit, and she would think that it was a rough draft. And she would write a chapter and give it to me, and she thought it was a message from Mount Sinai. So I couldn't touch hers, but she could rip my draft all apart. I write very quickly. She takes a long time. We didn't agree on a lot of facts of a lot of the stories. We each had our own memories of how those things went down. And it got to the point where we weren't speaking to each other and we would just send each other snippy little emails.

The Carters were ready to quit writing the book. The small disagreements turned into big arguments, which nearly destroyed their marriage. Their editor got involved, and he was able to take care of the chapters the two couldn't agree on, melding the versions. Because of the intervention, the book got written.

Diane Ream, the interviewer, asked, "You talk a lot about arguments that you and Rosalynn have had. Did you ever consider divorce?"

Mr. Carter waited about ten seconds and then said, "Yes, we did."

Then she asked why they didn't move forward with the divorce.

"Because we had made a decision in our life that every night we read the Bible together—one night she reads out loud and the next night I read out loud, and we pray. Whenever we would have a problem, we would pray, so we really did feel as though we never let things go too far."

Finding the strength in the solution is to make the perfect lemonade, especially when others add more to it than you want.

Ingredient six: Discover the good in the trial.

"Jesus loves you!" I heard someone yell.

I had an appointment with my physical therapist, who is helping me get back on the running trail. I pulled into the parking space just to the right of the front door, using my handicapped sticker. I put the van in park, shut off the motor, and glanced up to locate the magic button. I simply pushed the rectangular button and voilà, while I got out, the back passenger side door slowly slid back, the van lowered like a camel waiting for its rider to dismount, the ramp began to grind out of its hiding spot from under the van, and with a loud CLUNK it hit the pavement. The vehicle was now ready to release its precious cargo.

I bent in, pushed the red button that releases TJ's wheelchair, and caught him as he rolled down the ramp. I was just turning to close the door and make all the magic happen in reverse when I heard someone yelling something at me from across the parking lot. I looked over my shoulder to see an elderly gentleman standing by his truck. I yelled back, "I'm sorry, I didn't hear you!"

He then shouted again so I could hear him. "Jesus loves you!"

"Yes he does!" I smiled and yelled back.

That's what I get with my youngest boy. That's how people react to my beautiful son in his wheelchair. That's how people's hearts are touched by a visual reminder that life hands out sucky cards. That's the good that has come out of this trial.

My heart was touched on that day. God knew I would need strength to endure the hidden disabilities that touch my family. Those are the burdens that you can't smile about. You can only endure.

Lemonade isn't even my favorite drink. I rarely order it. But I love the analogy. One of my favorite quotes from a TV reality show is "When life hands you lemons, put nine in a bowl!" I love that. I love the humor. I love the idea that beauty is found in odd numbers, which is another analogy. Life can be odd; it is rarely even. Life isn't fair; only in grace can we find justice. Life is sour like lemons, and is only made delicious by adding something sweet.

Find your sweetener in your faith. Rise to your calling and your stewardship. Sister Sherry Dew reminds us, "I repeat that these are the days in which a true leader wants to live. These are days when opportunities to change lives and even destinies are nearly endless. You are running the anchor leg of the relay because you were born to lead. You were born for glory."

Make your lemonade your way and enjoy! Bottoms up!

CHAPTER 17

Turn on the Lights

I love the Pacific Northwest. On the few days that the sky is not a shade of dirty snow, the sunlight pulls you up and out like a starting pistol. In the spring, however, the cool, moist air chills you just enough to discourage leaving your warm bed. That is what I felt today. I would have stayed in bed all day, only rising to grab a bite to eat, served on a tray, if I still didn't have a child that I am responsible for. When most couples are celebrating having an empty nest, we will always have one little chick in ours. I am daily bathing, feeding, and changing diapers for an adult child who will never leave our home. Most days this fact I take in stride, but sometimes it's overwhelming.

I had made an appointment to have lunch with a friend but was considering canceling. I knew if I did, however, I would procrastinate even more about my dreaded daily routine. I needed some motivation to begin, and lunch was my motivation. I threw off the covers, swung my legs off the side of the bed, let out my morning sigh, and shuffled to TJ's room.

The minute I opened his door, he greeted me with a lip smack. That's his way of saying "I love you." Instantly my mood was lifted and I felt so rewarded for his presence and for this opportunity to serve him.

Bathed, dressed, and fed, we both headed out the door. The fresh air forced a deep inhale, and I took a quick glance up and around. Hmmm… it was a better day than I expected.

We headed to the mall; my friend and I agreed to meet at the food court. Not a romantic place or even a place to find good food, but it was close to her work and she had limited time. I got TJ's wheelchair placed near my chair and my friend and I chatted away.

My peripheral vision caught an orange-sweatered, baseball-capped gray-haired man and his family at the table next to ours. It was spring break, so the mall was filled with children, grandparents, and families of all kinds. Soon my friend and I said good-bye, hugged, and split right and left.

We were out of the house, and we were at the mall. What should we do now? Roam. So we meandered toward one end with not even a desire to window-shop but rather just a desire to not go home. We took the elevator down one level, and as we exited the lift and rounded the corner we passed the nice-looking grandparents who had been our neighbors at the food court. The orange sweater walked past me and we did the proverbial nod, the sign that reads, "I don't know you but we have been introduced through osmosis."

Before our shoulders were no longer parallel, the gentleman stopped and backed up. "Excuse me," he said. I stopped and turned to him. "I saw you upstairs at the food court," he said. I shook my head, embarrassed that we both knew that our eyes had met at one point.

"I told my wife if I saw you again I would stop and tell you something," he continued. "I want you to know that there is a protective aura around you. God is watching over you and your son and protecting you."

I thanked him, and with a nod, we parted.

My smile could have lit the entire mall. If it wasn't sunny outside, it was sunny in my heart. I'm sure other mall roamers may have wondered what was so funny as we continued our non-shopping.

This is my reward for often shuffling down the hall to TJ's room a little downtrodden. It gives me the strength to lift his twisted body; shave his handsome face; style his thick, wavy hair; force his stiff and bent limbs into currently stylish clothing; and take him out, share him with others. It's my job, I guess—my duty to share TJ with the world. He brings smiles to faces. He brightens lives and he doesn't even speak. He is my sunshine. He makes me and everyone he encounters happy when skies are gray.

However, there is another place I go to gain the feel of warm sunshine. In every LDS temple throughout the world there is a room where you can go to pray, ponder, and find peace. This room is usually entered after performing some sacred ordinance, and entering there is meant to conclude your service in such a way that you take the time to reflect on promises made or life-altering decisions, or to just meditate.

Every temple is decorated and adorned similarly but also is quite unique. In the Portland temple, the room is primarily cream-colored. Not stark white, but a warm, smooth, wrap-you-up-in-ivory-linen color. The sofas and chairs are covered in fabric that is formal and yet inviting. Tints and shades of yellow to soft gold are found in the window coverings, Carrara marble, and floral arrangements. The ceiling is high, allowing for a massive crystal chandelier. The fixture is gold with hundreds of prisms surrounding each flame-shaped bulb. In front of and behind this fixture that spans the upstairs sitting area and the downstairs, are two mirrors. They are identical and repeat the design found on the beveled white carpet on the floor. Repetition is found everywhere in this room. Repetition is one of the primary design elements in any room. This practice of repeating a shape, color, or line is what makes a room flow and appeal to our human eye. The huge mirrors combine flat sections with beveled, edged details. Stylistic floral petals top the flat surfaces on the bottom, with beveled panels in between each flat section on the top.

As I stood in that room one day, my eyes wandered from the gold-leafed borders surrounding the details on the ceiling to the reflections of the gigantic chandelier in the mirrors. My body began to sway as I saw that moving allowed my eyes to pick up the flashes of color and flicker reflected off the bent edges of the beveled, mirrored sections.

Even though this room is quiet, subdued, and monotonally neutral, the colors, movement, and fireworks being displayed were explosive. It was the epitome of symbolism that we are taught to look for. It was the visual description of every human who had walked into that room. It made me smile; it made me grateful; it filled another "Oh I get it" hole in my Swiss-cheese understanding of life.

"It takes all kinds," the mirror shouted at me. We must have flat, obedient, always-there-to-hold-you-up-type people in our world. We must also have slightly bent, a little on edge, and sitting-on-top-of-type people in our world to provide color, diversity, and challenges. Flat surfaces don't reflect color well but they do show us our reflection. Of course the image is reversed, as is so often our own. We need a little edge, a little color, a little fireworks to really see what we are made of—to bring out the pizazz, the sparkle.

We, too, need to deflect the white noise that is pushed into our ears, into our eyes, into our thoughts by the world's ideas. The prism we need in order to separate and reflect and push out rainbows comes in the form of crazy family members, hard jobs, sick kids, aging parents, instability, and evil choices. We hang these prisms all around the candle-shaped light called the Gospel, called the atonement, called repentance. What do we have then? A life filled with brightness and joy.

Just like the light I saw and felt in the House of the Lord, I can create my own massive chandelier, my testimony, lighting my upstairs and downstairs and all the stories of life, maybe even a basement or two.

You can do this, too. Find the light of love, joy, and laughter in your family. On hard days, get out of the house, create a fort in the dining room and have a picnic, or watch a funny video together. Your family needs you. They need the light of your love, even when it is hard to shine it. I leave you with this final quote from N. K. Jemisin in *The Hundred Thousand Kingdoms*:

> In a child's eyes, a mother is a goddess. She can be glorious or terrible, benevolent or filled with wrath, but she commands love either way. I am convinced that this is the greatest power in the universe.

ABOUT THE AUTHOR

René grew up in a small town just south of Chicago. Her childhood was filled with alternating snow and mosquitoes, corn, and family reunions. The only girl stuck between two brothers, she found sisterhood in her cousins.

She and her husband are the parents of six children and so far… thirteen grandchildren. René is a veteran of the US Navy where she served as a photographer. Her love of design and visual art led her to a quasi-career in interior design until the call of her true occupation, motherhood, demanded full attention. She and her husband live in the beautiful Pacific Northwest and take advantage of all it has to offer, including a great airport where they can leave the rainy weather occasionally.

Made in the USA
Columbia, SC
03 February 2022

55288157R00087